DRAWING CLOSER
TO
CHRIST

· · · · · · · · · · · · ·

DRAWING CLOSER TO CHRIST

A Self-Guided Icon Retreat

JOSEPH MALHAM

Photographs by Anna Marie Crovetti
Foreword by Most Reverend Robert Barron

AVE MARIA PRESS AVE Notre Dame, Indiana

To Fr. Paul Wachdorf

and all the people of St. Gregory the Great Parish,

who have given me the support, love, encouragement,

and home that has allowed me to respond

to my vocation these many years.

All scripture quotations are from the *New Revised Standard Version Bible*, copyright © 1989 National Council of the Churches of Christ in the United States of America. Used by permission. All rights reserved worldwide.

All interior and exterior photographs © 2017 by Anna Marie Crovetti.

Foreword © 2017 by Robert Barron

Founded in 1865, Ave Maria Press is a ministry of the United States Province of Holy Cross.

www.avemariapress.com

Paperback: ISBN-13 978-1-59471-757-4

E-book: ISBN-13 978-1-59471-758-1

Cover and text design by Katherine Robinson.

Printed and bound in the United States of America.

Library of Congress Cataloging-in-Publication Data is available.

CONTENTS

Plates fall between pages 50 and 51.

FOREWORD

The Christian artist builds bridges, and these bridges are routes of access to the beautiful, which is an evocation and expression of the reality of God. As such, artistic work is also in its own unique way priestly work; for the Christian artist who is faithful not only to his creativity and craft but also to the Lord entices humanity to consider their relationship to God and God's relationship to us. The artist does so by seeking to build bridges that gesture toward God's reality and presence or to accompany people along those bridges that God has himself built for us. While all artistic endeavors, enlivened by faith in Jesus Christ, can become an invitation to know him, it is the prayerful discipline of iconography that is an invitation to know Christ par excellence. Priestly work is prayerful work. The iconographer's fundamental task is not merely painting, but prayer.

Thus, the iconographer is not just the proponent of an artistic craft but a servant of the Lord. His or her method and medium is imbued with prayer, without which the result of the iconographer's efforts, though perhaps being stylistically correct, would become spiritually impotent. Thus, the task of the iconographer is the task to which all disciples of Jesus must apply themselves—namely, the death to self that manifests itself in a willingness to disappear into the mission of the Church. "He must increase, but I must decrease" (Jn 3:30)—this is what an iconographer must not only know but also be willing to do.

An icon is intended as an evocation not of the artist's personality and skill but of the heavenly reality that the icon represents. The iconographer is successful inasmuch as he disappears, standing aside so that the heavenly subject of the icon might be revealed. It is enough for the iconographer to be God's instrument. Let praise belong to God. Ultimately, the raison d'être for the icon is not the artist but what God has accomplished through his Incarnation—correlating in Christ divine and human, heavenly and earthly, invisible and visible. Pope St. John Paul II eloquently expressed in his "Letter to Artists" that "in becoming man, the Son of God has introduced into human history . . . a new dimension of beauty." Therefore, it is God in Christ who is the condition for the possibility of the icon. Without the Incarnation, the work of an iconographer would be merely a pretty curiosity. Because of the Incarnation, the icon is uniquely beautiful, and in its beauty, it is a bridge toward transcendence and a route of access to God.

For years, Joseph Malham has labored as an iconographer, living simply while unobtrusively embedded in St. Gregory the Great Parish in Chicago as an artist in residence. His work manifests his prayer, and his icons—while written in the midst of a contemporary, urban setting bustling with modern secularity—are ageless in their expressiveness, revealing the stunning paradox of the Lord himself who is ancient and yet forever new. While Joe is content to disappear into his mission as an iconographer, he is an outgoing, tireless missionary on behalf of the way of life embraced by an iconographer. He wants this way of life to be accessible, even if it can never be made easy. The Lord has given to him a gift that he believes will grow in proportion to his willingness to share what he has been given. Captivating others with the techniques he employs as an iconographer, he introduces people to the prayer that imbues his methods with sacred power, and in teaching people to pray, he invites people to know the Lord, not as a gilded totem, but as a living, divine person who wants us to know what he knows and love what he loves. Thus, Joe ventures forth along what Pope Francis refers to as the *via pulchritudinis*, the way of beauty. This way of beauty, as the Holy Father recommends, means showing that to believe in and follow Christ is not only something right and true but also something beautiful.

Drawing Closer to Christ is not simply a how-to manual, but it is an introduction to a way of life. This way of life enters into our world through the Incarnation of God in Christ, who invites us to partake of all the gifts and wonders he offers in the Church. As Christ is the Icon of the Invisible God, so his Church is the Icon of Christ, and the Icon of Church is revealed in a unique way of life. This way of life is, like God in Christ, good and true, but it is also beautiful. My hope is that the reader of this book will accept, as its author has, *the* way of beauty as his or her own bridge toward transcendence and privileged route of access to God.

Most Reverend Robert Barron
Auxiliary Bishop of Los Angeles
Founder, Word on Fire

INTRODUCTION

A shackled prisoner was sentenced to death but given a choice by his captors. He was taken into a silent courtyard and shown a foreboding black door. The condemned man had the choice to suffer a quick and relatively painless death by execution or to take a chance and enter through the black door. The prisoner, conjuring in his mind the potential terrors that might await him behind the dark portal, chose death by execution. After he met his fate, an eyewitness to the event inquired of the executioner: "Sir, what exactly is behind the black door?" The executioner stepped over, opened the door, and revealed the sun-drenched vastness of a glorious world outside the confining walls. "Freedom," he said.

So much of our lives as human beings, but more to the point as Christians, is spent resisting the invitation to that which brings greater freedom. Freedom from sin brings us back to union with the community (or Church). Freedom from our fears brings us back to union with the world. Freedom from that which holds us back from growth and conversion brings us back to union with ourselves. Freedom from all the above and all that is not good and life-giving brings us back to union with God.

Icons have experienced a phenomenal resurgence in Western spirituality, and what were once the ancient and sacred language of our Orthodox brothers and sisters are now an increasingly integral part of the faith journey for all Christians. Twenty years ago, the solemn, silent, and dark images of Christ, the Virgin, saints, and holy people were rarely seen outside of museums and art books, but today they are being engaged and venerated by more Western Christians. They pray with them, integrate them into their liturgies and sacred spaces, have them in their homes, and are moved to create them in workshops that are now being conducted all over the world. Why is that?

I believe that Western Christians have rediscovered icons not only for what they are but also for what they are not: museum pieces or dusty relics from an earlier epoch of faith, staring gloomily at us with large eyes darkened by centuries of soot, tallow, and the unforgiving effects of time. Instead, icons are living and vibrant testaments of faith, sacred portals through which God's truth and beauty shine forth into our realm and, literally, stare us in the face. The mystery is that, in total peace and prayerful repose, we can stare right back. It is the "beloved and lover" gaze of the Spanish mystic St. John of the Cross. It is the "I and Thou" dialogue of the Jewish philosopher Martin Buber. It is going through God's black door and falling in love.

If encountering icons—especially the Icon of the human face of God in the person of Jesus Christ—entails falling in love, then it stands to reason that we would want to know more about the One we love. If someone has an obsession with sailboats or speedboats, the logical impulse would be one day to attempt to drive one. If the obsession is light planes and the freedom of the open air, the impulse would be to take lessons to learn how to fly one. If someone begins to enter more prayerfully and intentionally into the mystery of icons, it is natural that the desire to create one would inevitably follow.

For nearly two decades as artist in residence at St. Gregory the Great Parish in Chicago, I have conducted more than one hundred icon workshops, retreats, lectures, and classes on the history and spirituality of icons. The most challenging (yet rewarding) have been the icon retreats, lasting from two to seven days, in which participants ranging in age from five to seventy-five journey with the Image. In the process, they encounter the Word, and ultimately they realize that the two are one. The problem that almost all participants encounter is not that of becoming proficient in iconography but that of simply beginning the journey. To return to the earlier story, fear and hesitation invariably hold them back. Only children, who are fearless, are without inhibitions and look forward to the opportunity to cover the panels and themselves with paint.

One of the first and most emphatic reasons adults give for why they can't take the icon workshop, despite their desire to do so, is "I can't even draw a stick figure!" What I don't tell them is, "Confidentially, neither can I." What I do say is that the reason for creating one's own icon is not to reproduce a luminous image that looks as if it just tumbled off the walls of the Annunciation Cathedral in Moscow. The reason for creating an icon is to embark on a journey, in prayer and silence, in which one will come to know intimately, not so much a process, but a person. This person may be Jesus, the second person of the Trinity; his Mother; or the men and women in the drama of salvation history who, like us, lived, loved, suffered, laughed, struggled, and ultimately became so absorbed in the life of God that his light came to shine through them. It is not our individual prowess that is being celebrated in the icon, but the triumph of those great lights that continue to shine in the Communion of Saints.

This book has been written to be your guide into the act of iconography, which is an act of prayer. It has been divided up into seven chapters, which not only measure the days it will take to create your icon, but also are an approximation of the days in which God created everything from nothing. Therefore, the creation story will guide this retreat. From the first chapter, where we will begin with a void and slowly create form, through the creation of light with the application of gold, to the use of water and pigments that come from the earth, we will slowly arrive at the fullness of the divinized person. We will not be simply painting as much as we will be actually participating in God's act of creation, which ultimately is the reason why we paint icons.

Everything you will need to know is in the book. This includes not only the step-by-step instructions but also reflections on the sacredness of each step of the process and materials. Also included is a list of all materials needed for the icon retreat, from brushes and panels to pigments, compass, and cleaning supplies (see page 112). If you are reading this book, it is because the Spirit has moved your heart to do so. Now we will begin to move your hands.

Guidelines

Before you start, however, here are some general guidelines to keep in mind.

- Remember that this is a retreat and not a work project with a deadline. Your seven-day retreat will be a fluid motion of prayer centered on the rhythm that you set. It is possible to work on your icon and complete several steps in one day or spread them out over several weeks. Our main objective here is not to be dogmatic with our "days" but to allow you the opportunity to enter prayerfully into the deeper meaning of each step along the way, becoming more intentional and aware of the work of your hands and the movement of the Spirit. Correlating each step with God's own work of creation, however long that took, is that for which we strive.

- This is your time, and your work area will become your "sacred space." Think of all the materials as the food that would be gathered when following a recipe for cooking. My mother, who was Greek and to whom cooking was as much a natural impulse as breathing, would say a prayer before putting bread into the oven and kiss the warm loaf as it was brought out. Like Brother Lawrence of the Resurrection, a seventeenth-century Carmelite writer, Mom gloried in the presence of God among her pots and pans in the kitchen. While I don't suggest (or even recommend) kissing your panel or jars of paint, an awareness of the sacred nature of your work will be reflected in the clear, uncluttered, almost Zen-like minimalism of your space.

- As you would if you were preparing to bake bread or a cake or make a full five-course meal for a special occasion, take the time first to read the list of materials needed for each day. Set before you only what you will need for that day's work in order to keep your space organized and "sacred" and not to be overwhelmed by the mass of materials and clutter that will inevitably crowd you. Keep the materials for the other days in a covered plastic storage box. If you are doing this retreat alone in the privacy of your room, chances are good that materials will become lost or shuffled around. If you are doing this in a school, a dorm, a parish setting, or a religious community, the chance of things getting scattered is almost inevitable.

- Carefully read the spiritual reflections and thoughts that precede the work section of each day. Understanding the sacred nature that underpins the steps of painting the icon will give you a better spiritual road map as to what you are doing and why.

- Also be sure to carefully read and reread the instructions for each step before jumping into it. Take a few minutes to practice on a sheet of clean paper or cardboard before you begin the actual work. For example, do some sample tracing with the carbon to see if you have the right sense of fluidity and gracefulness to the lines and curves of the face and garments. When it comes to the painting portion, practice with your brush to get a sense of control over painting, both the lines and the large areas that will be required. Also practice with the compass that will double as your paintbrush for doing circles.

- Clean and organize your area after each day's work. Remove any clutter such as paper, tape, and so on, and make absolutely sure that you wash all paintbrushes in warm soap and water and dry them gently with a soft cloth. Change your water daily, and have a steady supply of clean rags since you will probably use several during the painting process. Make sure all flecks of gold leaf are brushed up and collected in a small container for future patching or thrown away. Even synthetic gold leaf is not a good thing to have floating about and possibly ingested.

- Begin each day's work with a prayer. This could be silent prayer, or the morning prayer from the Liturgy of the Hours (the day's prayer can be found online), or a short reading from the New Testament. Close each day with the same. Bidden or unbidden, God is present, but it is an awareness of God's presence that we want to continue to heighten in our retreat as much as we want to do the same in the entirety of our lives.

Day 1

WORD AND IMAGE

The earth was a formless void. . . .
Then God said, "Let there be light";
and there was light.

~Genesis 1:2a, 3

When I was a novice in the monastery, I was brimful, as are most novices, with what is known in the trade as militant ignorance. Militant ignorance, in short, is when someone claims to know absolutely everything about things that in fact they know pretty much nothing about.

My militant ignorance in the novitiate revolved around my iconography lessons, which were being conducted by another artist named Joe. My greatest desire at the time was to be left alone so I could soar to the mystical heights of iconographic greatness without Joe looking over my shoulder. However, the minute he walked away, I became the equivalent of a three-year-old child in sandals and a black cowl, filled with abandonment issues and terrified of making appalling and irreparable mistakes that would simply ruin my icon in progress.

So it's easy to imagine the terror I felt when Joe told me that he was leaving for a two-week trip to Italy with his wife and that it was time for me to continue work on my icon alone—and without his constant assistance and calming presence. To me, that was the same as being adrift in the North Atlantic in a leaky lifeboat, with nothing but my terror, my icon panel, and my brushes. Joe, however, said something to me that I have carried with me for the past twenty-some years of painting icons and that I would now like to impart to you.

Joe told me, in effect, that if I calm down, engage my image, and enter quietly and prayerfully into the process, then, he promised, "the icon will tell you what to do next." Now, I had heard of weeping icons, bleeding icons, and icons that turned back armies and won battles for the soldiers who marched behind them, but I had never heard of a talking icon. Frankly, it unnerved me. It slowly dawned on me, though, that what Joe had been trying to instill in me was the mystery that I have endeavored to go into deeper ever since.

It is the leitmotif to which we will return again and again down the length of our retreat. What we are about to undertake is not a sort of spiritual Olympics; it is not a race we are running that is fueled by our own talents and that ends with a triumph based upon our own individual exertions. Instead, we are embarking on a journey into a relationship with the Other, a journey that entails an inner dynamic in which one speaks and the other listens and then vice versa. This is called conversation and, as a very wise priest friend of mine used to say, "wisdom is in the conversation." The conversation is part of the journey, and the journey is nothing more than a step-by-step process by which we arrive at a destination. In the end, what Joe was trying to tell a frightened novice shaking in his sandals was that while we do have maps and signposts pointing us in a particular direction, once we get into our rhythm, the act of going from step to step will become as natural and organic as putting one foot in front of the other.

Theological Reflection

"In the beginning . . . God created the heavens and the earth" (Gn 1:1). Not by coincidence, the first book of the Old Testament, Genesis, begins with the same words as the last of four canonical gospels, that of St. John: "In the beginning was the Word, and the Word was with God, and the Word was God" (Jn 1:1).

If we are setting out to learn the "how" of iconography, it is imperative that first and foremost we learn the "why." Why, of all three Abrahamic religions, do Christians dare to create images of the divine and pictures of the One who cannot be rendered in any visual form? Isn't that not only impossible but also an idolatrous and blasphemous violation of Mosaic Law?

We create icons and venerate them (but we do not worship them, which is widely and substantially different from veneration) because of one word: *Incarnation.* Of the three fragrant shoots of the Tree of Abraham and his One God, only Christians believe that God took flesh in the person of Jesus the Christ, the Messiah, the Anointed One, and, as St. John said, "lived among us" (see Jn 1:14). We believe that Jesus is truly God but also truly human, and that—like Shakespeare had Shylock say of himself in *The Merchant of Venice*—he was a Jewish man of the Law who had eyes, hands, organs, dimensions, senses, affections, and passions. In these ways, he was just like us. If killed, he would die, just as we would. Indeed, he suffered and died, but then he rose from the dead and broke forever the bondage of death. He ascended, still fully human and fully divine, to sit at the right hand of his Father. That is the Jesus we portray in iconography.

What has been clearly taught and understood in Eastern as well as Western Christianity is that images can be created of Jesus. This is because Jesus had a human body, and so creating and venerating images of him is a way of giving praise and honor to the Incarnation, the Word. We don't know how the Christians of the apostolic age and the subapostolic age, directly afterward, used imagery in worship, because the hard and fast data simply is not extant or conclusive. As the early Christians saw themselves as people of the Temple and continued to worship there, no images were used or even necessary, except perhaps the sign of the fish or the Chi-Rho (the monogram of Jesus' initials).

Later, as a fledgling sect spreading throughout the far-flung Roman Empire that embraced the known world, Christians began to assert their individuality and develop an iconographic language that by the second and third centuries was startlingly bold and pedagogically powerful. Though a bit rough-hewn, the catacombs of St. Callixtus in Rome (late second century) show how the Christians in the rapidly expanding Church were neither timid nor hesitant to portray Jesus, the Virgin, apostles, and scenes from scripture in the gathering spaces and burial *cubicula* (chamber or small room) of the dank, candlelit catacombs. The artisans employed a highly refined theology in their frescoes, showing Jesus as the Good Shepherd, Jesus with the woman at the well, Jesus raising Lazarus from the dead, and Jesus with his apostles at the Last Supper. Just as St. Matthew portrayed Jesus to his audience as the New Moses, the New Lawgiver, so also well-thought-out visual correlations in the catacombs show the finding of Moses in the water as similar to Christ's Nativity, the Crossing of the Red Sea as pointing to Baptism, and Moses striking water from the rock in the desert as compared to baptismal waters of life. Even at the dawn of Christianity, images were used not to decorate but to evangelize and to draw people deeper, through the surface reality, to infinite truths and riches beyond.

By the year 313, Christianity had been decriminalized in the reign of Emperor Constantine, and it was ultimately embraced by Theodosius I as the official religion of the Roman Empire in 380. The ancient center of power on the Tiber had fallen to the Goths and then shifted to Constantinople in the eastern fringes of the empire. Thus, under the emperors of Byzantium, who were the successors of Constantine and the old Roman Empire, icons were fully embraced as an integral part of the liturgy and spirituality of Eastern Christianity. They were seen to be as central to worship as the Cross and scripture, and the language and style became increasingly refined and more dazzling. Since Christianity was now officially married to the ruling dynasties and expressed the soul of an empire as well as a people, icons were now accorded the honor of being covered with gold, silver, and precious stones. Instead of being roughly rendered on cavern walls, icons were now proclaimed on more massive surfaces such as on the walls and domes of basilicas and in palaces, government buildings, and monasteries, as well as in the lowly homes of the lower classes. Despite their magnificence, the icons' simple message that the Word is also Image always remained firmly intact. It was the questioning of this truth, though, that soon led to the greatest challenge to the use of images in Christian worship.

Beginning in the eighth century and concluding in the middle of the ninth, Byzantium was sundered by the heresy known as iconoclasm. Influenced by certain bishops from Asia Minor, the Emperor Leo III (717–741) decreed that icons were idolatrous and blasphemous violations of God's law and ordered all to be destroyed. To the iconoclasts, only the Cross and the Chi-Rho were acceptable in public liturgy or private prayer. Suddenly, bishops, theologians, clergy, religious, and laity, men and women who for centuries saw icons as accepted and integral parts of their faith, now had to step forward and speak up in defense of the sacred images. Hundreds suffered imprisonment, torture, exile, and even death for the right to create and venerate their icons.

Out of this iconographic tumult, however, came forth some of the most powerful and profound theological defenses of the right use and understanding of images. The foremost theologian who defended icons during the heresy was St. John of Damascus (679–741), a fiery, uncompromising champion of the Catholic faith whose words still ring today with the courage of his convictions. Using the strength of orthodoxy coupled with good old-fashioned logic, St. John of Damascus neatly destroyed the iconoclastic arguments and clarified for all time the clear and distinct boundary between worship and veneration. When the iconoclasts charged that the Church faithful in the East were worshiping matter in the form of two-dimensional images of the Savior, St. John fired back. These Christians are not, John said, worshiping matter; they are worshiping the Creator of matter who became matter for their sake and their salvation. Never hesitant to kick a heretic when he was down, John further demolished the iconoclast's shaky logic by famously stating that, in the end, if one denies the image of Christ (which proclaims the Incarnation), one is actually denying the Incarnation. By the middle of the ninth century, the iconoclasts were completely crushed, and the use of icons was once, and forever, restored to their rightful place in Church worship in the East (the Church in the West had continued to support the use of images).

As we begin the journey of our icon retreat, let us look at both the previously mentioned scriptural passages from Genesis 1 and John 1 and the subject for our retreat: Christ Pantocrator—or Christ the All-Powerful, the Teacher. It is an image of the Lord of all that is, seen and unseen, who has conquered, not by the sword or great armies,

but by the fulfillment of the Law in love and the contradiction of the
Cross and empty tomb. Icons are windows, doorways, portals out of
our temporal realm and into eternal ones. They are objective truth
and, unlike secular art, not ends unto themselves. Icons guide and
teach. As visual manifestations of God's truth and beauty, they have
to be not only visually arresting but also theologically correct. Like
good liturgy, good ballet, and good art, the forms, gestures, colors, and
objects shown in icons all have a resonance and meaning that take the
viewer beyond the surface reality.

There is no description in scripture of how Jesus actually looked,
because physical details were not as important as his life and message. The earliest depictions of Jesus from the catacombs show him
as he would have been known to the Romans of the second and third
centuries: a clean-shaven young philosopher in a long toga, or a shepherd boy in a short tunic. By the fourth century, with Christianity the
official religion of a Roman Empire now centered in the East, the first
images of Jesus as a wisdom teacher with long hair and a beard began
to appear and then dominate in Christian iconography. This is the
template of the Lord that serves as our image of Christ Pantocrator.

Jesus, bearded and with long hair parted down the middle, stares
out toward us with large eyes that convey a sense of intimacy and
peace. He is clothed in garments that do not so much make an ancient
fashion statement as declare bold theological truths. Jesus' tunic is red,
while his cloak is a dark or purplish blue.

Remember that when icons came to mature use and widespread
veneration, the great number of faithful who encountered them could
not read. As Pope St. Gregory the Great said, images are books for the
unlettered. Therefore, the icons' symbols, gestures, and even colors
were intended to be read as though they were parchment scrolls in
order to be understood. When our Byzantine brothers and sisters
encountered the icon of Christ Pantocrator, in the dome of a basilica
or on a small panel hanging in their home, they could "read" the icon
in order to determine the person in the icon and establish a relationship and connection with the person whom the icon represents.

Red first connotes the idea of blood, that which gives our bodies
life and forms the physiological matrix of our humanity. In short, it

symbolizes humanity. The particular shade of blue in the cloak that Jesus wears drew immediate correlations with royalty, kingship, and divinity. Without dry cleaners and over-the-counter dyes in abundance throughout the ancient world, this shade of blue was achieved through the expensive, time-consuming, and no doubt unpleasant task of squeezing ink from shellfish. Thus, this color was reserved only for the most exalted ranks of those who could afford it—namely, royalty. Therefore, the combination of red and blue on Jesus' garments in the icon was to its first viewers, and still is to us, a declaration of Jesus' humanity and his divinity—the hypostatic union of true God and true man in one person. While to us this seems like an overstatement of the obvious, during the first several centuries of the Christian era, the Church was being rent asunder by the various heresies (like Arianism) that questioned the two natures in the one person of Jesus Christ.

Next the icon draws the reader to the hands of Christ. While his left holds the book of gospels (the Word of Life), his right hand is raised in a curious way that conveys both message and blessing. The fingers, crisscrossed over each other in what appears to be a confused jumble, are actually spelling out an abbreviation of the Greek initials for the holy name of Jesus (**IHCOYC**) Christ (**XPICTOC**). This is not a sign language but a sacred language that will speak to us, pointing to the Word who is, as God said of himself to Moses on Sinai, simply "I AM."

"In the beginning was the Word, and the Word was with God, and the Word was God" (Jn 1:1). The immensity of St. John's poetic prologue is no less daunting to get one's arms around than the opening verses of the first chapter of Genesis: "The earth was a formless void and darkness covered the face of the deep, while a wind from God swept over the face of the waters" (Gn 1:2). Even in the beginning, before time started ticking away in the vastness of space, the Word was.

We start with the preparation of our gessoed panel that is sanded on all six sides to the smoothest possible touch. A gessoed panel is basically a wood panel expressly prepared for the purpose of painting in a particular style or media—generally for egg tempera but also for oils and acrylics. Traditional gesso is made from a mixture of marble dust and watery glue from animal hides that, when applied in nearly a dozen layers, makes for a solid and sturdy "ground" upon which the image can be rendered. Unlike a canvas, with which an artist uses an underdrawing as his or her guide and visual road map, a gessoed panel can be etched with lines that allow the artist to see the placement of facial and garment lines when the opaque paint is applied in several layers.

By using a gessoed panel, we honor the preexisting Word, and the reason is twofold. First, as a gift of God's creation, which was spoken into existence by God's Word, wood is a sturdy and dependable material of great durability that is found aplenty in most parts of the world. Second, in using wood we honor the Cross, the means through which our salvation was achieved. The wood of the panel, even at this supposed state of "nothingness" and "void," shares by both its physical and its spiritual DNA a memory of Christ and his Paschal Mystery, and because of this we approach the material with reverence.

● ● ●

Painting the Icon

Materials for Day 1

- 8" x 10" white gessoed panel
- An 8"x 10" color copy and black-and-white copy of the Christ Pantocrator icon. You can obtain these images in two ways: (1) download and print both copies from the Ave Maria Press website at www.avemariapress.com/product/1-59471-757-5/ Drawing-Closer-to-Christ/#more_tab, or (2) photocopy Plate V of the color insert of this book in color and in black and white at 150 percent of the original. You will not trace the border so be sure to trim it from your black-and-white image.
- Carbon paper
- Adhesive tape
- Steel wool
- Ballpoint pen with fine point or fine-tip drafting pencil
- Compass with interchangeable pencil and painting nib (available at an art supply store)

Steps for Day 1

Step 1. First, take your steel wool and rub it over the white gessoed panel to give it a smooth shine. (See fig. 1.1.)

figure 1.1

Step 2. Place two images of the Pantocrator before you: the black-and-white photocopy and the full-color copy. Both images should be the exact same size of the panel but for different reasons. The black-and-white copy will be used to transfer the image (that is, to trace the image from the black-and-white copy onto the gessoed panel), and the color photo will be your painting guide for the icon.

Freehand tracing is possible, but even the great artists of the Renaissance did preliminary drawings, called cartoons, which would be laid upon the wet plaster of murals through which holes and charcoal dust would be inserted in order to give outlines on the wall. For our purposes, we will use the same process of the transfer but with the modern convenience of the clever little invention called carbon paper.

Take your sheet of carbon paper and place it on the panel, carbon side down and tracing side up. One sheet should suffice for your panel, but if it is smaller than the panel, simply center it with equal amounts of white panel showing on all four sides.

Step 3. Then take your black-and-white photocopy and place it face up over the carbon paper, again centering it on the panel so it is flush with the four sides or so there are equal amounts of white panel showing on all sides. Take three pieces of adhesive tape, and tape the photocopy and the carbon paper to the panel on the top and the two sides. (See fig. 1.2.) This will ensure that neither pieces of paper shift or slide about during the tracing process. Lines that are broken or

figure 1.2

misaligned are to be avoided at all cost, or the icon could become a Cubist or abstract painting.

Step 4. When your photocopy is securely taped to the panel over the carbon, you are now ready to begin the tracing and transfer process. Select a ballpoint pen with a very fine point or a clickable drafting pencil, likewise with a very fine lead tip. Avoid using a standard No. 2 lead pencil or even a fine-tip felt pen, as those will not give you the pressure needed for a dark, crisp trace through the photocopy and carbon paper.

Instead of jumping around from section to section of the image and getting lost or retracing traced lines, start with the overall outline of the head and body and slowly work your way in. Select a point on the top of Jesus' hair and, exerting a uniform pressure (neither too hard nor too light), work your way down one side and then down the other side. From there, move inward to the outlines of the hair (including the lines that form and separate the strands) and the hands before moving on to the details on the face.

Continue with the folds of the garments, paying close attention to the individual lines, which are striated and stylized, and may resemble masses of sculpted stone rather than the flowing and naturalistic cloth of oil paintings. (See fig. 1.3.) To avoid becoming confused and seeing the lines like the old Roman Pitchfork optical illusion (either seeing

figure 1.3

three individual prongs or seeing the spaces between, which make it five prongs), reduce the masses to individual forms. One swirl of garment folds may resemble a calla lily, another may look like a long inverted spoon, while the shadows could resemble letters of the alphabet. Seeing them as forms will give an organic flow to your tracing and will reduce the stress of having to "get everything right."

Step 5. When you have finished the body, head, hair, face, book, and garments, be absolutely sure to trace the halo, the significance of which will be discussed in Day 3. While you still have your carbon underneath the photocopy, trace the line of the halo from point to point by drawing only spaced dots and without yet drawing a curved line (which you will do in step 7, after the carbon paper is removed). (See fig. 1.4.) You will not get an exact circle by tracing freehand. Only a few artists throughout history have been able to do this, and, believe me, I am not one of them.

figure 1.4

Step 6. Before removing the photocopy and carbon paper, be absolutely certain that all the lines have been traced, to the smallest detail, on the panel. A good way to tell is to hold the panel up to the light, and you will see the metallic reflection of either the pencil lead or the ink. When you are satisfied that you have covered all the lines, slowly remove the tape and peel off the photocopy and the carbon paper to reveal the drawing—your drawing. (See fig. 1.5.)

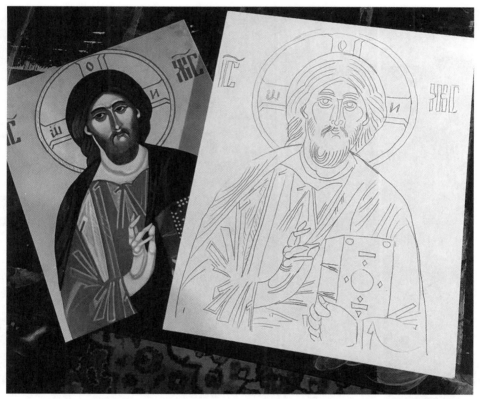

figure 1.5

Step 7. Next, take your compass and find the center on the face of Christ, which generally is the bridge of the nose.

    With your compass set at the center point on the bridge of the nose, open the compass for a few twirls in the air above the surface of the panel, and shift the point until the traced dotted circle and the compass circle match. Then put the pencil down and draw your halo circle around the head. (See fig. 1.6.)

figure 1.6

• • •

Remember that the lines of an icon, like its gestures and colors, join together in a graceful way and, like a ballet, point to meanings, emotions, and realities deeper than the visible surface. Even at this early stage of the journey, keep in mind that there is no step greater or lesser than another. The tracing is not merely a mechanical task to finish quickly in order to get to the more important step of the actual painting. Throughout the process we are mirroring the days of creation, and just as every stage of God's creation of the universe explodes with cosmic significance, so also should we work with intentionality and consider the importance of each step. With that in mind, be aware of the movement of your hand, and let your pen or pencil trace over the lines with a balletic and poetic fluidity.

And there was evening and there was morning, the first day.

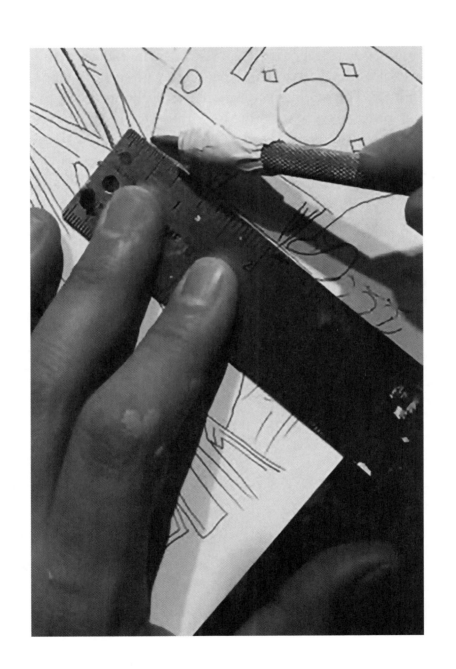

Day 2

DIVINE SON

*And God said, "Let there be a dome in the midst of the waters,
and let it separate the waters from the waters." . . .
God called the dome Sky.*

~Genesis 1:6, 8a

One fine summer day, when I was twelve, in what was without doubt the shortest agricultural career in history, I was picking ripe apples off the trees on our family farm outside Chicago. Theoretically, the apples would be gathered in our ancient root cellar and would end up as pies, apple sauce, or snacks in our kitchen. Sometimes, they would be sold to unsuspecting motorists tooling up and down Miller Road.

Somewhere during the picking process, my apple gathering became woolgathering, and the thought occurred to me: Where does the universe end? Even if, I thought, the universe extends to the very limits of space, doesn't it hit some sort of galactic firewall and suddenly end? Even if it does, I thought, something would have to be on the other side, and then where did that space end? While not exactly Newtonian in its profundity, my scientific inquiry into the ultimate frontiers of time and space became as painful as my apple picking, and both endeavors were soon at an end.

Theological Reflection

The answer for our purpose here, at least for an iconographer, is not to be found in astronomy, quantum physics, or the study of black holes. Instead, our purpose is described in the prologue of the Gospel of John: "To all who received [the Word], who believed in his name, he gave power to become children of God" (Jn 1:12).

The most poetic part of the most mystical of all the canonical gospels is an ancient Christological hymn to the preexisting *Logos*, the Word, of God: "In the beginning was the Word, and the Word was with God, and the Word was God. He was in the beginning with God. All things came into being through him, and without him not one thing came into being" (Jn 1:1–3b). In short, and unlike the created universe, John's prologue sings the theological truth that Christ always *was*.

Even the poetic language of John's prologue cannot obscure the unequivocal and immutable theological truth being proclaimed— namely, that the Son existed from all time with God in a singularly and uniquely filial way. This theological truth was declared throughout the New Testament. St. Paul, in his Letter to the Colossians, echoes John's prologue when he writes that "[Christ] is the image [Greek: *eikon*] of the invisible God, the firstborn of all creation" (Col 1:15). Jesus made this same declaration about himself, again in the Gospel of John, when he was asked if he makes himself out to be greater than Father Abraham: "Very truly, I tell you, before Abraham was, I am" (Jn 8:58).

This declaration is not merely an affirmation of an obvious existential state. Jesus is not simply saying that he is a living, breathing, walking, and talking entity. He is using the same words in reference to himself that God said to Moses about *himself*: "I AM" (Ex 3:14). In effect, Jesus says that he is not merely *a* being but in very truth the very *act* of being (Latin: *ipsum esse*) and therefore without beginning or end. The unprecedented and shockingly powerful nature of these words was not lost on John's Greek speaking audience. In fact, it wasn't lost on Jesus' hearers either, as immediately after he said this, the crowd picked up rocks with the intention of stoning him to death (see Jn 8:59). Never before had a son of the Law put himself on such equal footing with God, and doing so understandably put not a few nerves and teeth on edge.

This may seem like so much theological hairsplitting and semantic swordplay, but it goes to the very heart of who Jesus is. While our intention here is to demonstrate *how* to paint icons, the whole endeavor is rather futile without a crystalline understanding of *why* we paint icons.

While God in his essence can never be imaged in any shape or manner, is Jesus both truly God and truly man? And if he is indeed God in flesh, can that flesh be imaged and reverenced? To all the above, the Arians, among others, declared a vociferous and unequivocal *no*.

Of all the heresies that rocked and sundered the Early Church, none was more famous, widespread, and toxic as the Arian heresy. Named for the teachings of Arius, a fourth-century presbyter from Alexandria, the heresy was a rather large umbrella under which gathered Christians who affirmed the reality of the *Logos* but denied the divinity of Jesus. God, the Arians taught, is so unknowable, vast, and untouchable that he could never deign to befoul himself with corrupt human flesh and remain God. While Arianism did not specifically target the question about icons and categorically condemn the use of images, the heresy did open up the door to more direct attacks in the future.

Jesus of Nazareth, so they said, is the greatest creature made by God, the foremost human being in all history worthy of dignity and honor. He was not, however, uncreated and preexisting, nor did he share the same substance of God from all eternity. The Arians taught that the man Jesus, in his flesh, was not divine and that visible flesh was nothing more than an instrument, a useless adjunct that hid the true *Logos* in all his unknowable glory while being the mouthpiece of God's message. Like a flimsy toolshed, hastily thrown together to house valuable tools through the winter, the man called Jesus was an insignificant bit of housing. Just as a toolshed would be torn down in the spring and the material would disappear back into the earth, so the Arians believed that Jesus the man was simply subsumed into the glory of God after his death on the Cross. Icons of Christ, therefore, are not only useless but pointless as well.

Eastern Christians had to fight long and hard for the right to create icons that are proclaimed as manifestations of Jesus who is both truly divine and truly human in one person. The iconographic struggle, however, has extended into a long and ongoing fight to keep and maintain this "right praise" in the core beliefs of Christianity itself. That struggle continues even now.

While the Arians were attempting to contradict what the early Christians thought about Jesus' two natures in one person, there was another group of theologians, armed with ironclad faith and irrefutable logic, who were waiting for them around every corner. These towering minds and souls of the Early Church, collectively known as the Church Fathers, included such theological giants as Athanasius, John Chrysostom, Basil the Great, Gregory of Nyssa, and Gregory Nazianzen. Perhaps most vociferous on the subject was St. Cyril of Jerusalem, bishop and theologian. These men were all staunch and eloquent proponents of Christ as God in the flesh and were not shrinking violets when it came to striking back at the Arian heretics.

Cyril of Jerusalem (AD 313–386), an unflinching verbal pugilist who pulled no punches when it came to heresy, was also a deeply sensitive pastor when it came to the proper education of catechumens endeavoring to seek and follow Christ. Cyril first and foremost used the words of scripture, both those said about the Lord as well as those said by the Lord himself, to prove that Jesus was indeed God in the flesh. In his eleventh catechetical conference, Cyril said that even before the commencement of Jesus' ministry, the heavens opened and the voice of God declared, "This is my Son" (Mt 3:17). Later, he repeats as a catechetical leitmotif what Jesus said of himself to Philip at the Last Supper: "Have I been with you all this time, Philip, and you still do not know me? Whoever has seen me has seen the Father" (Jn 14:9).

Using the subtle nuances of theological and philosophical Greek like a paring knife, Cyril proceeded to expose the illogical nature of the Arian arguments with unerring accuracy. At the heart of his argument is the difference between being God's children by adoption, as we are through our baptismal immersion into the passion, death, and resurrection of Christ, and being actually begotten by God, as is only the one Son of God, Jesus. God, Cyril pointed out, did not say to Jesus at his baptism: "This is *now* my Son," or, "This one has *become* my Son." He said: "This *is* my Son." While Cyril says that we are all begotten of water and the Spirit, reborn and made new, Jesus alone was begotten of the Father, by the Father, and as such existed from all time with the Father. Parrying the weak arguments of the Arians with the strength of his, Cyril says that God did this without ceasing to be God, or becoming two Gods, or even lessening his infinite glory and majesty. Jesus, as the *Logos*, the Word and Son of God, was begotten perfectly in a way known only to God. As Jesus iterates and reiterates again and again in the Gospel of St. John, the Father is in the Son and the Son is in the Father. The Son radiates the glory of God the Father, and the Father flows through the Son, two but one, as rivers flow unto the sea.

For Cyril, and indeed for all the Church Fathers, it was a matter of logic that proved Jesus was truly God in true flesh and blood. God does not do half measures, nor is he half-present anywhere in heaven or on earth or in the farthest reaches of time and space. The Arians believed that God could not become true human flesh and still remain God. Contrarily, the Fathers riposted, when God took flesh for the one and only time, he, by logic, inhabited that flesh entirely and completely— otherwise, it stood to reason, he would not be God. It is the same as saying that God created the earth but, since he could not reduce his glory by fully inhabiting the earth, it is a transparent, pointless, and ultimately useless world. We believe with St. Francis of Assisi that the earth is sacred and our mother, brother, and sister because it was created by God and reflects the wonder of his beauty. In the same way, we honor all humanity as created in the image of God. For our purpose and intents, we take things a step further and say that we honor the icon of Christ and reverence it because it is a created reflection of the human face of God in the flesh.

That posture, that crystalline understanding of Jesus as God in the flesh (and not a temporary toolshed), is both the starting point and catalytic agent for our first step in rendering the image of Christ. Before proceeding pell-mell into the fray, however, take some time to enter prayerfully into this mystery. As you cannot hope to finish the icon in one day, so do not expect to plumb the depths of this eternal mystery with any immediate and satisfactory results. Do not try to solve the mystery, but enter into the mystery. We are embarking on a journey with a person, not an object, and one of the most fruitful and satisfactory things that can happen to us is to get to know someone along the journey, whether it be a day on a train or plane or a lifetime with a friend or spouse.

The act of creation, as well as the Father's continual act of begetting the Son, is first and foremost an act of love. In both instances, while the act itself is a mystery, the fruit does indeed have a face. Let us continue.

• • •

Painting the Icon

Materials for Day 2

- Needle-pointed stylus or fine-tip incising tool
- Ruler

Steps for Day 2

I am often asked in my icon workshops or lectures the same question: "Is it possible for someone to create an original icon bearing his or her own unique personality and style, or is each icon merely an impersonal copy of a copy of a copy?" That question, quite frankly, begins to be answered at the stage where we now find ourselves. As you proceed, you will find that the more you work in a spirit of silence, prayer, and listening with an open heart, you will discover that what is unfolding is not an aesthetic process but the evolution of a relationship. You are not simply learning how to paint an icon but are slowly coming to know an Other. Like all relationships, it involves patience, time, hard work, self-emptying, and, most importantly, listening. Without fail, listening, more than speaking, helps to resolve conflict, banish hesitation, lift fear and anxiety, and, as if you were a lost tourist, helps you understand where to go next. In this present journey, listening is essential because you are being called into a deeper relationship with Jesus through the intimate yet measured process of revealing his face as you write your icon. This listening and personal relationship with Jesus infuses the icon with your spiritual DNA and thumbprint.

This could sound like so many pious platitudes were it not for the fact that this is true on a technical and mechanical level as well. Regardless of whether you are creating this icon alone or in a group with twenty other people, this stage is the critical juncture where the icon becomes indisputably yours. I will shortly explain.

As I indicated above, whether this is being done alone or in a group, it is impossible for any two of the drawings to be exactly alike. Pressure, fluidity, and a host of combined elements of the tracing has rendered your panel truly and uniquely your own. Like we pondered in the mystery of the Father and the Son, they are the same, as it were, and yet wholly other. In this next step, where you will etch the image into the wood, the image will become even more uniquely your own.

Now that we have our traced image transferred to the panel, we proceed with extreme caution and awareness to the next step: the etching of the image into the panel with a stylus. (See fig. 2.1.) The reasons for caution are not only that the stylus has a sharp point but also

figure 2.1

that you do not want to run the risk of smudging the carbon tracing on the panel. Remember, just as your incising is only as good as your drawing, so will your painting be only as good as your lines. Unlike painting on canvas, painting on wood panel is basically an opaque process, and once the first layers of paint go down, the underdrawing will completely disappear. The lines you etch will shortly be your road map, your guide to every line on your image from the eyes, mouth, and fingers to the folds of the garments. How fine your icons become hinge upon how thorough and complete are your lines.

Step 1. As with the tracing, begin the etching with your stylus at the top of the head, and work your way down along the outline of the body. Move inward and etch the individual lines of the hair, eyes, nose, mouth, shadows under the eyes and around the nose, mouth, temples, and cheeks. (See fig. 2.2.) Although it may appear to blend into the shadows of the neck, trace the outline of the beard as well.

figure 2.2

With the same poetic fluidity you used with the tracing, etch in the lines around the fingers, the details on the book, and all the delicate folds and striations of the outer and under garment. Use a ruler to incise the straight lines of the book and the gold band over Jesus' shoulder lying on his red tunic. When incising, don't feel as though you are sculpting stone or cutting through ice. A nice, thin line using uniform pressure to avoid jagged and zigzagged lines will more than suffice. Even the lightest of lines will surprise you in how visible they remain even under several layers of paint.

Step 2. Two little tricks can be employed to tell you if you are etching the lines properly. The first is the furrow. Etching into a gessoed board is very much like pushing a shovel through fresh-fallen snow, since when you run the incisor over a line, a small furrow of white powder will arise on either side of the line. When you can blow off powder after cutting in a line, you know you are cutting properly.

The other trick is the click. Most of the carbon tracing of the image will disappear as you incise the lines, but it is probable that several lines, all of them essential, will be missed. To ensure that you have etched all the lines, simply take your stylus and run it gently over the surface, one section at a time. You should hear the tip of the stylus making clicking noises over the lines. If you hear the clicking, likewise you will know that the lines have been cut.

● ● ●

The image has been transferred and the lines have been incised, and you are now ready to apply the gold leaf of the halo and the color for the background on the next day. Look and see how good it truly is.

And there was evening and there was morning, the second day.

Day 3

THE ETERNAL

And God said,
"Let the earth put forth vegetation: plants yielding seed,
and fruit trees of every kind."

~Genesis 1:11

In the 1948 action-noir classic *The Treasure of the Sierra Madre,* director John Huston brilliantly and insightfully examined the corrosive effects of gold on men's souls and the extents to which people will go to possess the shiny stuff.

Three destitute and desperate prospectors set off into the remote mountains of Mexico to find gold, all the while pledging eternal friendship, loyalty, and fraternity with each other. No matter what woes come their way, they swear, nothing will break their bond of devotion. However, as the gold begins to pile up and their prospective wealth increases, so does their suspicion, animosity, and paranoia.

The crusty old veteran of the group keeps talking about an inherent evil that inevitably follows when men strike the mother lode—and sure enough, suspicion leads to hostility, hostility leads to madness, and as sure as night follows day, madness leads to murder. *The Treasure of the Sierra Madre* is ultimately an ageless fable, a universal and enduring lesson that warns against the evils of lust for gold, wealth, power, and all that leads humanity to try to be like God.

Theological Reflection

Since time immemorial, gold has had a particularly powerful allure for humanity, and it has come to symbolize power in almost all civilizations from ancient Egypt, Greece, and Rome to the pre-Columbian empires of the Aztecs and Mayans. Gold, more than anything produced on or pulled from the earth, dazzles the eye, scintillates the soul, and conveys the impression of permanence, transcendence, and immortality. However, as with almost everything else we human beings think we understand about God and eternity, we're not even in the ballpark.

If gold automatically connotes Babylonian visions of fabulous wealth and everlasting glory, for our purposes it means something entirely different. In iconography, the gold used on the surface of the panel, but primarily on the halo and the background, represents the true splendor and eternal radiance of God's uncreated light. This is a light that is both overwhelming and terrible in its magnificence and also strangely elusive for human beings to fathom. This is not merely because, as human beings in this world, we cannot see the glory of God's face in eternity, the Beatific Vision, as do our loved ones who have died in the peace of Christ. It is also because of the ultimate limits of our ability to imagine eternity and the concept of light without a created source.

Just imagine, all our light—from the sun to a candle, with everything in between from electric bulbs to our cell phones—emanates from something that has been created. To read the words in this book, you are using natural sunlight, light generated through bulbs, or, for the most wildly romantic, light from a candle or blazing fire. Regardless of the source, it all comes from some original and created point.

Now, try to imagine passing into the eternal realm and into the actual presence of the living God. There is no sun, there is no fire, and it can be said with a fair measure of certitude that there are no light bulbs or cell phones. In the heavenly presence of God, you will be dwelling in light—perpetual and uncreated blazes of unspeakable brilliance that, because time there does not exist, will simply *be*. Where does this light come from? Naturally, from the almighty and eternal

God who is not merely the source of this light but, more importantly, is the very essence of uncreated light.

When I was a novice in a monastery for several years, the most beautiful and peaceful of all the hours of the Divine Office was, at least to me, the office of Compline, the final office (meaning a set time for prayer) for the day. The other offices of the day all had their beauty, profundity, and resonance for their particular hour of worship. Morning prayer, sung at the break of dawn, roused us from sleep, and as we gave thanks to God for the gift of another day, this prayer helped us to welcome the sun (symbolic of Christ) that would be the source of our light as we set about our work. Midday prayer at noon was a sort of spiritual coffee break, a respite from the work that refocused our hearts and minds on the fact that everything we did was for the glory of God. Evening prayer, like all the hours of the Divine Office, mirrored the cycle of our daily lives. Like evening itself, it sung about the need to wind down, rest, contemplate the good and bad we did during the day, and prepare for the coming night.

There was, however, an entirely different feeling and texture to Compline: a sweetly mystical touch that was as all-enveloping as the embrace of night itself. The reasons, again for me at least, were twofold. The first was that Compline was sung when the church was bathed in almost complete darkness, except for the few lights needed to read our psalters and a few candles flickering around the icon of the Theotokos, the Mother of God. It was an omnipresent reminder that, in life and in death, the Virgin is our Mother. Not coincidentally, that maternal element of the prayer gave Compline an almost lullaby-like quality, a rocking song to put us to sleep as the darkest part of night approached.

Second, Compline sings the songs of the sweet slumber of eternity and a remembrance of our final end. However, before you think that this concept was intended to scare the young novices into a state of anemia as well as insomnia, let me point out that what emerged from this poetry is the idea that death is not like going through a black door. On the contrary, it is like an infant, reposed in peace and trust, falling asleep in its mother's arms. The prayer that closed Compline was a passage from the book of Revelation: "And there will be no more night; they need no light of lamp or sun, for the Lord God will be their light, and they will reign forever and ever" (Rv 22:5). Because Christ's death has vanquished death itself, the light of God's face will welcome us into the eternal glory of his reign and will transform us into light itself. And that is the meaning of the gold that will be placed on the icon you now have before you.

• • •

Painting the Icon

Materials for Day 3

- 4 or 5 sheets of gold leaf (real is best, but imitation will suffice)
- Gold size (gold-leaf glue)
- Extremely soft, imitation sable brush (for brushing, not painting)
- Compass with painting nib
- Steel wool
- Utility brushes:
  - Medium round brush
  - Small flat utility brush
- Painting brush:
  - Fine dagger-point liner brush
- Plastic or paper utility cups (about 3 ounces)
- Squirt bottle filled with water
- Fine-grit sandpaper
- Plastic palette with at least 6 to 8 "wells"
- Clean rags
- Scrap paper
- Liquid acrylic paints (1 ounce each):
  - Venetian Red
  - Cadmium Red
  - Burnt Umber

Steps for Day 3

Now that we have a crystalline understanding of the role of gold in iconography, we are ready to proceed with the ancient process known as gilding. The act of gilding is about as old to civilization as is the taste of water. It is indigenous to almost every culture and epoch and has decorated everything from Aztec pyramids and Greek temples to the palaces of the Russian czars and the hallowed halls and monuments of America.

There are two methods of applying gold leaf to a surface: water gilding and oil gilding. Both are intense processes requiring a tremendous amount of patience, concentration, and, for reasons you will soon discover, a complete absence of wind and breezes.

Water gilding is the more appropriately ancient of the two methods since it also requires the semimystical powers and skills of the ancients to effectively pull it off. Months, sometimes years, of practice and trial and error is required to perfect the water-gilding technique. Basically, it employs a process of laying down, one at a time, single sheets of loose gold leaf that are pounded and hammered thinner than tissue. With specialized tools such as a pad, knife, agate stone, and thin "card" brush with a single line of long hairs, the leaf is cut, whisked up via the static of the brush hair, and quickly applied to a thin layer of water on top of polished red clay called bole. If you are a bit bewildered and terrified so far, don't worry. Gilding is merely another part of the icon-painting process that, once done, will become easier and more enjoyable in the future. At the exact moment of dryness (if the water under the leaf is too puddled, the leaf will tear and disintegrate, and if it's too dry, the burnishing will not work), the gold leaf is lightly massaged with uniform pressure with an agate stone, millimeter by millimeter, which slowly transforms the gold from a dull yellow to a blazing translucence. However, given our time and experiential constraints, we will stick to oil gilding for our icon.

The art of oil gilding requires, as its name suggests, a thick medium inserted between the gold and the panel. This substance is a gluelike, premixed solution called gold size. This will be used, in lieu of water, to make the leaf adhere properly to the panel. In the water-gilding technique, a red clay is used under the gold to give a nice cushion substrate upon which the gold leaf can sit and be burnished. We will not use red clay but red acrylic paint. While we will not be burnishing, the red paint will act as a chromatic cushion of sorts that will give a nice warm hue to the gold leaf. Because gold leaf is almost transparent, it tends to look a bit tinny and yellowy when it sits on plain white panels. However, when gold leaf sits on a dark red foundation, something mysterious happens. A rich warmth and a mellow, tawny hue is introduced that dovetails perfectly with the overall mystery of our journey.

Step 1. You will remember that during Day 1 we traced and then drew the halo around Christ's head with a compass. With your compass and its painting nib (into which paint can be applied in order to paint perfect circles), find the center of Christ's face and open the compass to the exact size of the etched-in halo. Since we will be laying down opaque paint and will lose the halo lines, knowing the exact size of the halo is absolutely essential. When the compass is opened to the exact size, lay it aside and make sure it stays opened as you paint.

Step 2. Take one of your plastic or paper utility cups, and fill it a little less than one-fourth full with your Venetian Red paint. Since the paint may come out with the consistency of sour cream, take your squirt bottle and give a few squirts of water to thin it out to the consistency of heavy cream.

Step 3. With a small flat utility brush, begin applying the first of at least two to three coats to cover the area between the halo edge and the head with a nice even red surface. (See fig. 3.1.)

figure 3.1

Be sure to brush out all ridges of paint with the soft sable brush, since even the slightest imperfection on the surface of the panel will show through the gold leaf. If a few still appear after it is dry, sand them down with your fine-grit sandpaper. (See fig. 3.2.)

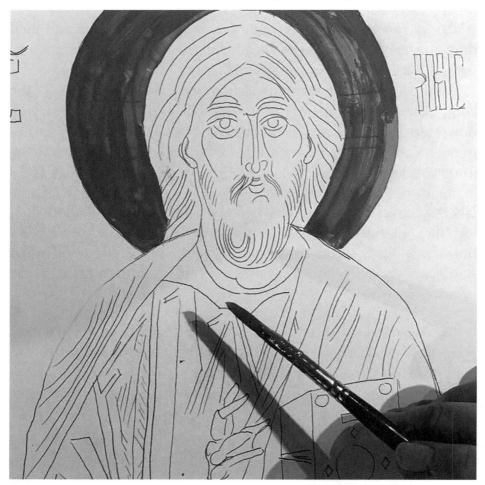

figure 3.2

Let the paint thoroughly dry in between coats because any moisture in the layers will cause some mischief later on. A good test is to touch the layer when you think it is dry. If it feels as if it's at room temperature, then it is dry; if it feels even the slightest bit cold, then that means there is still moisture in the paint.

Also, be sure to cut in close around the body and head of Jesus; clean, crisp, and sharp edges may require the services of a fine dagger-point liner painting brush. Even at this point (a leitmotif to which I will return again and again), it is important to be continually aware of your lines. If you want to lay the foundations of becoming a good iconographer, and I say this without a hint of sarcasm, you must become proficient at making your lines tight, straight, crisp, and intentional. Since iconography is an organic as well as a spiritual process, everything will flow, as it does in prayer, from your awareness, your focus, and your intentionality.

Step 4. When you have laid down at least three coats of Venetian Red that have completely dried, take your fine sandpaper and sand the red paint smooth and free of all dents, lines, and ridges created by the brushing. Any flaws, down to a single brush hair, will be noticeable through and indeed amplified by the gold. When the Venetian Red is smooth to the touch and your fingers do not feel any lines or ridges, take your steel wool and give the painted panel a once-over, as you did the white panel, so that it has a smooth shine and glow. You are now ready to apply the gold leaf.

Step 5. Again taking a clean utility cup, and this time fill it about one-fourth full of gold size (you can pour more in and return any excess back into the bottle). With your clean, small flat utility brush, dip into the gold size and apply it in nice even strokes to the entire surface of the Venetian Red. Like painting the red itself, cut in along the outline of Jesus' head and body with a fine dagger-point liner brush, making the finest and sharpest line without any unevenness. (See fig. 3.3.) Remember, your gold leaf will go wherever your glue is applied, so keep the lines neat, even, and on the red.

figure 3.3

One evenly applied coat of gold size will suffice, since applying more than one coat will make the surface extremely thick, glutinous, and lumpy. When dry, the gold-sized portion of the panel should resemble a placid, waveless surface of a pond. Hold the panel up to the light to ensure that there are no dry bald spots and that there is one uniform layer of gold size. If there are any bare spots, simply brush them with gold size and wait for the spots to dry. Like water gilding, oil gilding has a specific window of optimal time to apply the leaf. If the gold size is too moist, the gold will slosh around and tear; and if it is too dry, the gold will not adhere and simply flake off.

Since I have already given out numerous trade secrets and ancient tricks, I will let you in on another to see if your gold size is properly dry and ready for the gold. Close your middle finger and run the middle knuckle backward over the size. You should feel a slight resistance and hear a squeaking noise. One of the continuing leitmotifs on our journey is a realization of the difference between moving fast and moving with deliberate intentionality. The former allows your haste to defeat your purpose, while the latter allows you to move swiftly and steadily because you know what you are doing. That's a big difference, so move forward with confidence while working through your fears and hesitations. (See fig. 3.4.)

figure 3.4

Step 6. Our purpose is to maximize the area of panel gilded within the shortest time frame while wasting as little gold as possible. With these three cardinal rules in mind, take your first square tissue of gold leaf, and line it up as flush as you can with the top left corner of the panel, gold side down and the tissue side up. (See fig. 3.5.)

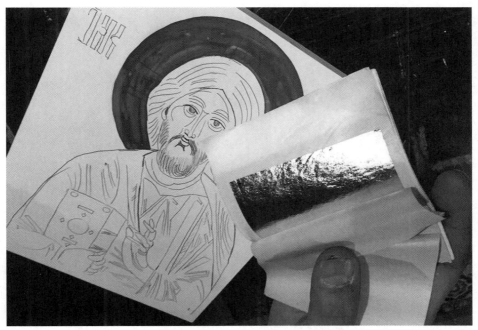

figure 3.5

With a uniform pressure (do not tap as though you're sending Morse code through the leaf), glide the pad of your forefinger over the entire surface of the square until you are certain that all the gold has adhered to the red halo area. (See fig. 3.6.) After a few more passes with your finger, slowly peel the tissue back to reveal the first fruits of your gilding.

figure 3.6

Step 7. Lay the next sheet down beside the one you just affixed to the panel. You don't want any red showing between the sheets, so instead of trying to get each sheet flush with the other, lay it a bit over the last one (just a millimeter or so), and continue to do so with the next gold sheets. (See fig. 3.7.)

figure 3.7

Step 8. It won't be long before you get the rhythmic feel of the gilding process, so proceed to the next sheet as quickly as possible. Let nothing go to waste on the sheet (remember, it is gold), so use any portion of the sheet that was left over from the previous application in the next one. As you come to the section around the outline of the hair and body, be certain to get every indentation and curve where there is gold size. Turn and angle your sheet to ensure that every single piece of gold leaf is used, and feel free to turn the panel around as well; it is an organic process, so don't feel constrained or bounded by propriety. This is your icon, so be comfortable and even intimate with it.

Step 9. When the entire surface of the panel that was formerly covered with Venetian Red and gold size is now covered with gold leaf, there is still more work to be done before we finish with the gilding stage of our day. There will be raised lines and jagged remnants of the gold leaf left as the sheets were pulled up. These lines need to be brushed and smoothed. (See fig. 3.8.)

figure 3.8

To make sure that the gold is not scratched, use the extremely soft imitation sable brush, and gently begin to brush the ridges away, as well as any stray particles on the rest of the panel. (See fig. 3.9.) Be gentle and patient with this last step, and appreciate the fact that no matter how much you brush and brush, raking light will still reveal more particles of gold leaf. These particles, no matter how minute, will find their way into wet paint if they are not removed, and they will then become impossible to pick out. Brush several more times, and then take a soft cotton rag or towel (do not use paper towels, since these are synthetic and will scratch the surface) and lightly run it over the surface of the entire panel to remove any remaining particles.

figure 3.9

Step 10. Now that your surface is gilded and fleck-free, use the painting nib of your compass and mix a small combination of Cadmium Red with a dollop of Burnt Umber (brown) into one of the wells of your plastic palette. Add a bit of water to make the paint mixture, again, the consistency of heavy cream. If it is the consistency of milk, it will drip out of the nib onto your panel, and even gently dabbing with it will cause it to leak into and stain or even rub through the gold. If it is too thick, like sour cream, it won't flow through the nib. When it is the right consistency, take a medium round utility brush, dip it in the red paint mixture, and transfer the pigment into the nib by simply brushing it alongside the two open prongs above where they come together. (See fig. 3.10.) The pigment will fill up the nib, but to

figure 3.10

be sure that it will not drip on your panel, hold it over a piece of scrap paper. If it does not drip, put the needle point on the scrap paper, and trace one or two practice circles to get the feel for and control of the paint flowing through the nib.

Step 11. Refill the nib with the paint mixture in the same way as before, and with the needle point of the compass, find the hole previously made on the bridge of the nose (from when you used the compass on Day 1 to draw the halo). Lightly touch the nib to the panel's surface to start the paint flowing. Then highlight the outer edge of the halo (but not the inner edge) by placing the nib down just below the shoulder line and gently moving the compass in a circle over the head and just below the other shoulder line. When you have your halo completed, lift the compass and be very careful not to touch or smudge the wet lines.

Step 12. Leave the icon aside for the day. We will complete the cross and inscription inside the halo later.

• ○ •

It has been a good and productive day with new and ancient skills examined and performed. Wait for nightfall, and close out your day by praying Compline. If you do not have a breviary, it can easily be found on the Internet. Pay close attention to the verbal images of night, darkness, and how the gloom of death has been destroyed by the blazing glory of Christ's Paschal Mystery. Contemplate the darkness of our lives and how the darkness will be forever vanquished, and instead our lives will be eternally illuminated when the light of God's face will become all in all, which means that there will be no separation of God from fallen humanity, and all will be gathered up into that light for all eternity. Look at your icon and see that it is good.

And there was evening and there was morning, the third day.

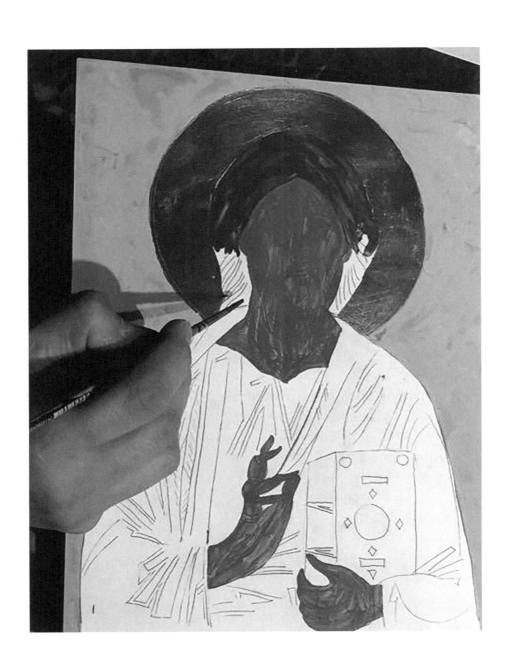

Day 4

LIGHT IN THE DARKNESS

*And God said, "Let there be lights
in the dome of the sky to
separate the day from the night."*

~Genesis 1:14a

One of the most sublime, fascinating, and utterly poetic mystics in the history of Western Christianity is, without doubt, the diminutive and captivating Spanish Carmelite friar St. John of the Cross (1542–1591). John was a brilliant, yet controversial figure in his own time, due mainly to the reforms of his Carmelite order that he enacted with his good friend St. Teresa of Avila. Far from being a detached ascetic with his head in a "cloud of unknowing," John was also a scholar, poet, spiritual director, artist, amateur architect, and religious superior known for his wisdom and common-sense approach to religious life. Despite all this, John continually ran afoul of his own superiors and confreres and would have been banished to a foundation in Mexico had he not died at the age of forty-nine.

Within a few years of his death, however, the majestic beauty of his poetry and the sublimity of his teachings was ultimately recognized throughout Catholic Europe. He was canonized in 1726, and in 1926 he was declared a Doctor of the Church with the singularly honorific title "The Mystical Doctor." Even though John wrote letters, aphorisms, and instructions to young novices, he is best remembered for his extraordinarily beautiful poetry and accompanying explanations. In fact, John is widely considered one of the greatest poets to have written in the Spanish language. When one reads his poems, even in a language other than Spanish, the reason quickly becomes clear.

The foundation for John's poems was laid when he was forcibly taken to Toledo and imprisoned in a dark closetlike cell for nine months when he refused to abandon his proposed reforms. In the terror, isolation, and loneliness of that world of endless night, John had a revelation that pierced to the core of his soul. John understood that unity with God is not always achieved through light, clarity, and a complete understanding of the intellect. The realm of light is the realm of the senses, and both are fallible and limited by an existential firewall beyond which we simply and ultimately cannot pass. No matter how far our minds extend to the limits of human thought, there is a point when our senses finally stop and surrender to mystery. We can only truly begin to know God, John says, in darkness.

John's masterpiece, which is probably his best known and most beloved poem, is "Dark Night of the Soul." Often mistaken as the psychological state of depression brought about by catastrophe or overwhelming misery, the dark night in fact refers to the soul's journey from our ideas of what God is to actual union with God as God is. This journey entails passing from light and understanding and pleasurable sensations of love and consolation to a place beyond all human knowing and comprehension. This state, into which John says we must enter "in nakedness and night," is called the dark night. It is in this darkness and night that the soul finds unity with the One she loves.

John was a brilliant man who was steeped in a scholarly knowledge of sacred as well as secular writings. He based his dark night on the Old Testament's Song of Songs as well as medieval Spanish romances and ballads. The beginning of both the Song of Songs and the poem "Dark Night of the Soul" are explicitly bridal and sexual and speak of the passionate longing of the young bride for her elusive groom. Searching in the dark of night for her beloved, the bride finds the One she loves; and lying in each other's arms in the bedchamber, the two sleep as one forever in a state of united bliss.

Theological Reflection

Why have we chosen St. John of the Cross to be our guide for this particular step of the journey? The first and foremost reason is that between the magnificence of his verse and the wisdom of his counsels, John is an evergreen spiritual master for all seasons and all peoples of faith. More to our purpose, however, is John's illumination, as it were, of the concept of darkness and night and our journey to unity and fulfillment through trust and faith alone. What is integral not only in John's poetry but also in his overall mystical theology is the idea that in order to advance in our unity with God, we must leave behind all that we previously understood to be the beautiful, bright, and consoling dimensions of God. Like a child weaned from its mother's breast, we must begin to eat solid food, and instead of being carried, we must stumble and struggle to walk on our own.

This letting go of our comfort zone, our sense of certainty, and all that we perceive as perfection is particularly resonant at this stage of our icon-painting journey. Even though you may be new to the iconographic experience, by now you will have started to feel the beginnings of a rhythm. It's similar to that seminal moment of riding a bike for the first time and not tumbling to the pavement, jumping into a pool and actually swimming rather than sinking like a stone, or playing a guitar or piano and feeling the tune flow through your fingers as music. For the first time you feel that you are engaged in a special endeavor that is pulling you in deeper and deeper.

Right now your panel, clean and bright, is resplendent with an etched image that bears your own artistic and spiritual DNA. Not only that, but also it bears the glory of a gold halo that you applied using ancient techniques and materials. However, like John's verse regarding the soul's journey to God, we must now leave the comfort of what we know and can control and enter through "nakedness and night" into the dark night, flying blindly by faith and trust alone. We are now about to mess up our world and lay down the first of numerous layers of paint that will obscure our own etched lines, obliterate what remains of our drawing, and plunge our icon into what will look like a dark and inscrutable morass. With complete trust and confidence

in our etched lines and our ability to patiently bring forth the light,
we move into the shadowlands of the image, guided only by John's
"ray of darkness."

• • •

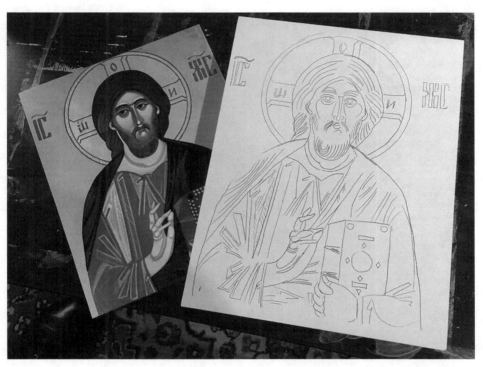

Plate I (fig. 1.5 on p. 13).
The image of the Christ Pantocrator, traced with carbon paper on to
wood panel, ready for incising.

Plate II (fig. 5.2 on p. 67).
Scumbling the first layers of the flesh highlights.

Plate III (fig. 5.9 on p. 74).
Close-up of the garment highlights.

Plate IV (fig. 6.4 on p. 90).
Close-up of the facial details.

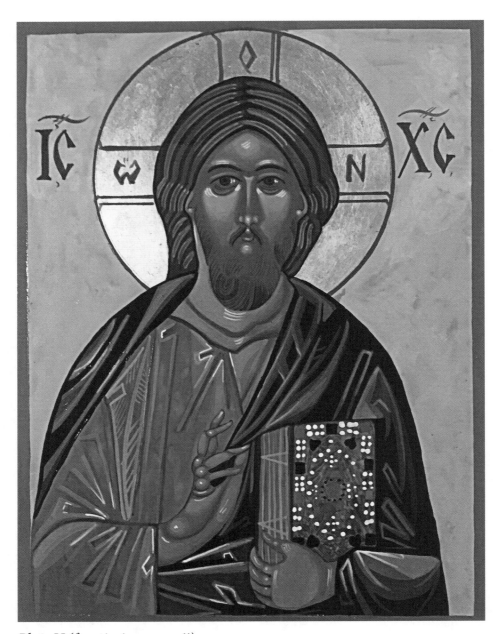

Plate V (frontispiece on p. ii).
The completed icon of the Christ Pantocrator.

Painting the Icon

Materials for Day 4

- Painting brushes:
  - #8 large round brush
  - #4 medium round brush
  - #10 small round brush
  - Fine dagger-point liner brush
- Liquid acrylic paints (1 ounce each):
  - Yellow Oxide
  - Raw Umber
  - Titanium White
  - Cadmium Red
  - Burnt Umber
  - Black
  - Prussian Blue
  - Yellow Ochre
- Plastic palette with at least 6 to 8 "wells"
- Squirt bottle filled with water
- Plastic or paper utility cups (about 3 ounces)
- Clean rags
- Plastic wrap

Steps for Day 4

In order to begin the process of illuminating the icon, we must start by reducing every area of color to its darkest value. For example, the blue robes of Jesus will be painted indigo, his tunic will be dark burgundy, the book will be brown, and so forth. However, the first color field to be applied is the background of the icon. Unlike Western sacred portraits, Eastern icons do not employ backgrounds that hint at a naturalistic setting in real time and space. There are no blue skies with clouds, no pastoral landscapes, and no church spires to frame them in a geographical context. We use a theological rule of thumb that applies to both the halo and the entire background: it is not so much a place as it is a spiritual reality. The glory of God's uncreated light not only surrounds the one shown but also permeates and radiates him or her from within.

Step 1. So that we can keep the creation of our image on the economic side, we will forgo the use of real gold on the entire background and instead opt for a painted yellow field. Take one of your utility cups and fill it about one-fourth full with Yellow Oxide paint. Add three to four drops of Raw Umber, one to two drops of Titanium White, and a few squirts of water from your bottle to give the paint mixture the consistency of milk (we want it more watery than the consistency of heavy cream that we wanted previously). Mix the paint well, making sure to get any stray pigment on the bottom of the cup, and you are ready to apply.

Step 2. Take a medium-size round painting brush (not the cheaper utility brush this time), and dip it into the paint, making sure to get the "load" of paint in the bristles without immersing it up to the wood. With nice, even strokes, apply the base layer to the background by using long sweeping strokes in an up-and-down fashion. Make sure that there is an even coat over the entire panel with no bald spots, and paint in any that may appear. Then wait for the paint to dry.

Step 3. To give some texture and depth to the background so that it's not just a solid yellow, we are now going to add several successive layers of brighter and more watery coats. To do so, add two to three short squeezes of Titanium White paint into the yellow pigment as well as about one-fourth of a clean utility cup of water to the solution. Mix well, and then with your largest round brush, apply the paint over the yellow in even strokes, allowing it to puddle as it resists the base coat. This is what you want because when it dries it will appear as areas of cloudiness, almost as if it has been marbleized. (See fig. 4.1.)

figure 4.1

Step 4. For the final coat, add another two to three squeezes of white and another one-fourth utility cup of water to the paint, and mix it to a thoroughly milky color and consistency. This time you want to apply it while the last coat is either fully wet or even partially wet. As the moist layer pulls and separates, it will create a lovely kaleidoscope of color patches with the same result as mixing oil and water. (See fig. 4.2.) If some spots are still wet, all the better; that pooling will lend to the swirling organic patterns. Use the same large round brush to apply the paint to the background in even strokes, and then let the paint dry.

figure 4.2

Step 5. When the background color has completely dried, you are now ready to start laying down the base colors of the face, hair, garments, and book. As we get to the humanity of the icon, bear in mind what we said about illuminating the icon from darkness to light. We are going to start with colors reduced to their darkest values without actually going to black.

As we are not painting large fields but are now concentrating on smaller areas in which we will be building up forms, switch to your paint palette tray with its six to eight individual cups. In one of these cups, begin to mix the paint for the face of Jesus. Squeeze in Yellow Oxide three-fourths of the way to the top, followed by one-fourth Raw Umber, leaving a bit of room for the water you'll need to thin it out with. It will be a yellowish-greenish mixture, an organic earth tone that we want as our base as though we were drawing from the clay of the earth itself. However, to warm up the flesh, put in a small drop of Cadmium Red. I say a small drop since, due to the high concentration of pigment in this color, a little bit will go a very long way. A dollop on the tip of your brush should do it nicely. Mix everything up well with a clean brush, remembering to get any stray paint on the bottom, and add a few drops of water until it is the consistency of heavy cream. Remember to clean your brush between each color change. Think of washing your brushes after painting as being as important as washing your hands before eating.

Step 6. When the paint is thoroughly mixed, take your medium-size round brush and apply the paint, evenly and smoothly, over the

entire facial area, paying extremely close attention to the smoothness of the paint and the crispness of the sections as you paint them. Even though your etched lines will guide you, it is best to get into the habit of disciplining your hand. Also, make sure that the etched lines are all visible under the paint. (See fig. 4.3.) If they are not, you may want to reincise them deeper before any other layers of paint go down. Remember to

figure 4.3

remove any ridges or creases created by the stroke of your brush. You will be putting down lines, and your intention is to be as intentional as possible. Apply at least three coats of the flesh base color, allowing each one to dry before applying the next one.

Step 7. Continue on to paint both hands with the same paint mixture. The left holding the book is a large and well-defined field, but the right hand of blessing is more intricate; therefore, feel free to use your smaller, fine liner brush to make sure all the fingers are covered.

Step 8. Make sure each layer is dry to prevent any moisture remaining under the surface. When the third layer over all the flesh portions is dry, use another palette cup to fill it three-fourths full with Burnt Umber (the dark brown, not to be confused with the greenish Raw Umber) and one-fourth full with Yellow Ochre (not to be confused with your Yellow Oxide). Squirt in the amount of water needed to get the consistency of heavy cream, and mix thoroughly.

Step 9. With your medium-size round brush, use your mixture to paint Jesus' hair, paying close attention to the clean roundness of the outside lines and not forgetting that the hair goes down the side of the neck and behind the shoulders. Remember to use your color photo to ensure that you don't miss any areas. After at least three coats (four if there are any white or bald spots showing through), allowing each one to dry before painting the other, let Jesus' hair dry. (See fig. 4.4.)

figure 4.4

Step 10. Since we want to paint the garments as they are put on, Jesus' red tunic will come first. Red, as we said before, is a densely pigmented color, but for our purposes it needs to be brought down to a darker value so as to be brought up again to a lighter value later.

To give it the proper darkness as well as to ensure the opacity, mix into a palette cup three-fourths Cadmium Red with one-fourth Burnt Umber and a very, very small dollop of Black (which is obviously even more densely pigmented than Red), and mix in some sprays of water to achieve the consistency of heavy cream.

Step 11. To ensure that you have enough opacity, put down three to four layers in even strokes on the red tunic area, using the color photograph as a guide, and letting each layer dry before applying the next one. Be sure to smooth out the creases and ridges, and check for any white patches or bald spots. Also be aware of your etched lines, and make sure that they are all visible under the paint. (See fig. 4.5.) If they are not, you may want to reincise them deeper before any other layers of paint go down.

figure 4.5

Step 12. In yet another palette cup, mix three-fourths Prussian Blue and one-fourth Burnt Umber with another very small dollop of Black and a few squirts of water to achieve the heavy-cream consistency. (See fig. 4.6.)

Step 13. With a clean brush, thoroughly mix the blue and likewise paint in the area of the outer garment, using even strokes and letting each layer dry before applying the next one. Blue, especially when mixed with another dark color, is particularly opaque and will go down very dark, but still be sure

figure 4.6

to apply two to three coats to ensure the proper amounts of layers are down. (See fig. 4.7.) Bear in mind the need to be ever vigilant about the crispness of your lines; getting into this habit in the large areas will

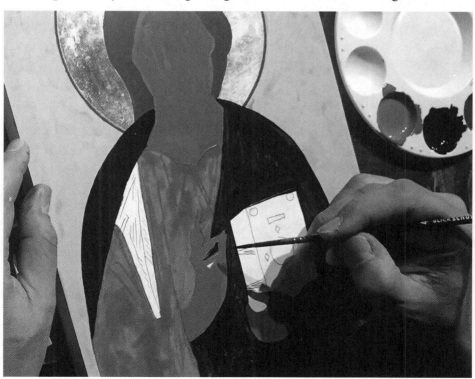

figure 4.7

prime and prep you for the fine-detail lines of the face and garments later.

Step 14. To finish our day's work, let us focus now on the small but key image of the book that Jesus holds in his left hand. The book of gospels, which is closed, may seem a bit anachronistic since the gospels did not exist at the time of Jesus as we now know them—they were first written down about twenty or thirty years after the Resurrection. The book is symbolic not only of Jesus as the Word but also of Jesus' supremacy as the Pantocrator, the Teacher.

For the book cover, take three-fourths Burnt Umber and one-fourth Yellow Ochre and mix them well in a clean palette cup, adding water so that it's the consistency of heavy cream.

figure 4.8

Step 15. Now with your small round painting brush (not the fine liner), apply three to four coats in even strokes (letting each dry before applying the next one) to the book cover. Obviously, the lines for the book represent an object and not the organic outlines and curves of the hair and robes. (See fig. 4.8.) Pay extremely close attention to the outlines of the book cover. A good trick to use, especially for the straight lines on your icon, is to employ the lines you cut in over your drawing. While they don't appear to be deep chasms, they actually are deep enough to act as a miniature trough to catch the paint exactly where you cut them. Push the paint to the etched line, and it will drop in. The etched line acts as a catch basin of sorts, giving you the line exactly as you cut and etched it.

Step 16. After the layers of brown for the book cover have dried, mix just the reverse amount of the same colors, placing three-fourths Yellow Ochre in a palette cup and adding one-fourth Burnt Umber. Mix well, and add a few drops of water to achieve the consistency of heavy cream.

Step 17. Use this to paint the pages of the closed book. Two to three coats should suffice (allowing each one to dry before painting the next one).

Step 18. After this, thoroughly wash your brushes with warm soap and water, gently rolling them around your soapy palm in order to get out all the pigments that have saturated the hairs. Dry the brushes thoroughly. Since you want to save the paint upon which we will begin to build brighter values, add a squirt of water to each of the cups in the palette that contains paint. This will prevent them from drying out and will ensure a base color for several days. After doing this, cover your palette with the plastic cover that came with it or a sheet of plastic wrap (not aluminum foil) to ensure that little to no air gets inside. Organize and straighten up your work area so that you come to a clean and ordered space the next day.

● ● ●

When you have finished these chores that will be repeated after each day of painting, look and see how good your icon is.

And there was evening and there was morning, the fourth day.

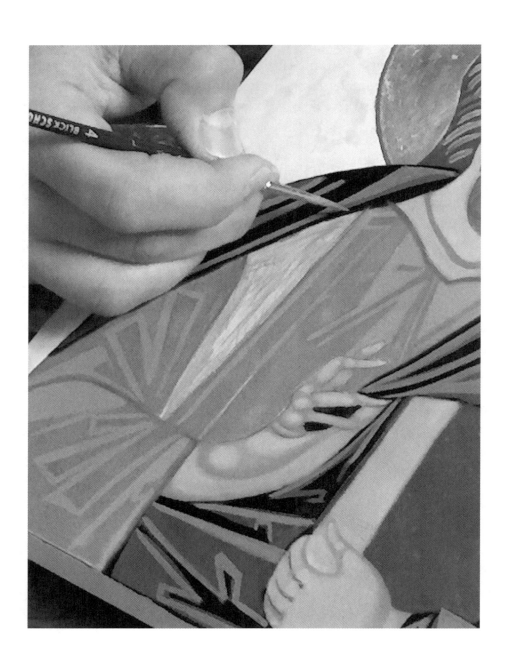

Day 5

Of all the religious films chronicling the lives of the saints, none evokes a more immediate response, good or bad, than Franco Zeffirelli's 1973 *Brother Sun, Sister Moon*, a biopic on the early life of St. Francis of Assisi. Depending on who you ask (and the mood they are in), the film generally evokes one of two responses. Either it is a moving and poetic celebration of the life of the *poverello* of Assisi, beautifully scored and wonderfully photographed on location in Umbria, that is both spiritually exhilarating and artistically sublime. Or it is a piece of 1970s revisionist claptrap, a smarmy and syrupy mess that reduces one of the Church's most beloved and prominent saints to a hippy-dippy flower child and history's first middle-class dropout—a complete fabrication, they say, that glosses over seminal moments in Francis's early life while omitting large chunks of his later life. Being the wild and incurable romantic that I am, I tend toward the former as the better and even more realistic portrayal of Francis and the transformative effect of God's grace in his life. That sounds a bit paradoxical and, like most of what I say, needs a bit of explaining.

The Zeffirelli biography of St. Francis does not purport to be an accurate and historically correct portrayal of the youth and early religious life of Francis any more than *Lawrence of Arabia* is an accurate portrayal of the founding of the Middle East states or *Gone with the Wind* is an accurate portrayal of the Civil War and Reconstruction periods. Anything that vaguely endeavors to be seen as art begins that process by intentionally taking those who encounter it beyond the surface reality into places deep within, where something will be revealed. What will be revealed is not just about the work of art but about the person portrayed, about humanity, about the world, about our place in the universe, or about God. This is not achieved through hard facts and cold data but through poetry, color, gestures, and emotion—fleeting flourishes of beauty that express an inner truth through exterior forms. In that sense all films, art, great works of music, poetry, and literature are icons.

In the Zeffirelli film, after returning home wounded from war, Francis opens his heart to God's love and grace, and his conversion happens in the most innocent and innocuous of ways. He follows a small sparrow from his sickbed out onto his roof and is literally transfigured by the radiance of the morning sun. From that point on, the film is no longer draped in a dark, grayish gloom but becomes suffused in a warm glow of sun-dappled pastoral beauty as Francis wanders through the hills of Assisi. Everything, from the grass and flowers to the butterflies and sheep, glows from within with a new divine light. Even the large crucifix that hangs in the crumbling church of San Damiano, which Francis gazes upon, radiates from within as it speaks to the depths of Francis's soul and tells him: "Go rebuild my Church."

Theological Reflection

When we open our hearts and turn from all that is not good, God's ineffable peace creates within us a stupendous light show—a mystical *aurora borealis* begins to explode in and around us. Not only do we see the world surrounding us and everyone in it set afire, as we do when we fall in love, but now emptied of all that is not God, we ourselves become conduits and vehicles of light.

By now you probably see where we are going with this slightly protracted meditation and how it pertains to our icon. Like Francis after his conversion, we do not simply see the world as it is in its natural, physical state. We see people, trees, flowers, rocks, water, and air itself remade and lit from within with the fire of the Incarnation, the Word made flesh. We see all creation, especially people, made new—brought forth from the darkness of death into the light of life and grace. We must be careful, however, to have a crystalline understanding of this spiritual reality. It is important to distinguish between honoring creation as a reflection of the Creator and worshiping matter itself.

I need not emphasize the fact that we are not animists. We do not look at the sky, mountains, trees, stars, sun, or even animals and worship them as divine entities in themselves. Like Francis, we behold the luminous beauty of God's creation and sing the "Canticle of the Creatures." We give thanks to God for the beauty of his creation and commit ourselves to cherishing and protecting the earth as a reflection of the Maker's love and beauty. This exaltation of God's creation is worthless unless we understand the distinction made by St. John of Damascus. We remember, from Day 1, his answer to the iconoclasts who claimed that champions of icons blasphemously worshiped matter. We do not worship matter, John said, but the One who became matter for our salvation. Let us continue.

● ○ ●

Painting the Icon

Materials for Day 5

- Painting brushes:
  - #4 medium round brush
  - #10 small round brush
  - Fine dagger-point liner brush
- Liquid acrylic paints (1 ounce each):
  - Yellow Oxide
  - Raw Umber
  - Titanium White
  - Cadmium Red
  - Burnt Umber
  - Black
  - Prussian Blue
  - Yellow Ochre
- Plastic palette with at least 6 to 8 "wells"
- Squirt bottle filled with water
- Scrap paper
- Clean rags
- Plastic wrap

Steps for Day 5

As we begin the journey from darkness to light in our icon, bear in mind that you will see a transformation that will be stunning but gradual. Prepare to spend many hours with your icon at this stage, since the layers you will apply will be numerous, perhaps as many as twenty, and you will need to allow a sufficient amount of time in between layers for drying. Instead of drumming your fingers, blowing on the panel, or checking your email and cell phone while you wait for it to dry, go deeper into the silence with prayer. Embrace the quietude, both exterior and interior; light a candle, put on some soft classical music or Gregorian chant, or even grab a little snack or tea to keep your energy up and your mind focused.

In order to achieve the gradation from darkness to light and light to darkness required for the flesh, hair, and garments, we will use a variation on a painting technique called scumbling. Scumbling is a method of painting in which thin layers of pigment are fanned out over other layers while allowing the bottom layers to still shine through. It can be a fairly difficult technique to master at first, but if you diligently and patiently stay with it, a rhythm and flow will emerge and give you increased control over your icon. However, more important than having control, you will endow your image with a grace, subtle beauty, and glow, and by mastering this gradual transformation from darkness to light, you will enrich your own spiritual journey.

Step 1. We will start by turning our attention to Jesus' hair. The mass of dark hair cannot be painted strand by strand; not even the greatest of Renaissance painters attempted that. Like everything else in your icon, the hair is stylized and painted to reflect an inner illumination rather than an exterior light source. Take the dark brown base pigment you initially used for the hair, which you have (hopefully) covered and saved from the previous day; the palette cup should be around one-half full. Add three drops of Yellow Ochre and one drop of Yellow Oxide as well as a squirt of water to thin it to the consistency of heavy cream.

Step 2. With this brighter pigment, take the medium round painting brush and paint a line thinner than each strand made by the etched lines on either side, so that you create thick, individual strands beginning at the center of the parted hair on top, continuing around the curve of the face and ear, and then following the thick round curls around the neck and shoulders. By creating these almost tubular forms, these "ribbons of hair" with a thick dark shadow in between, you will begin to create the impression of thick strands flowing down in a fluid manner following the curvature of the head and neck. (See fig. 5.1.) Two to three coats should do (allowing each to dry before applying the next one). Then thoroughly wash your brush.

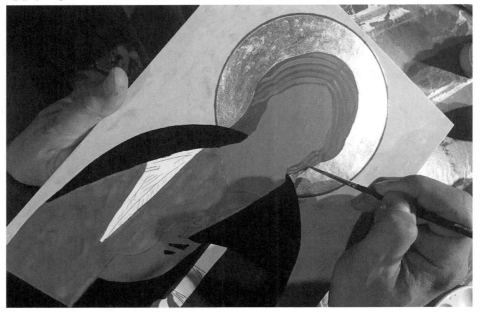

figure 5.1

Step 3. We will now move on to the face. Take the mixture of flesh tone that you have saved from the previous day; the palette cup should be around one-half full. Fill it nearly to the top with Yellow Oxide and add one small drop of Titanium White and then a dollop of Cadmium Red from the tip of your small round painting brush. Mix well and add the squirts of water to bring it to the consistency of heavy cream.

Step 4. Although I will do my best to describe the scumbling technique, it is ultimately grasped when, like music and rhythm, it is felt rather than explained. With that in mind, take your small round painting brush (not your fine liner brush), and dip it well into the flesh pigment. Then wipe off all excess paint on the side of the cup lip. Beginning with the brightest spot where the corner of the lower left eye and the cheekbone meet, do not stroke as much as gently scrub the paint in a circular motion, creating a bright spot and scumbling the paint down until it runs out and blends in with the darker color below. What you are doing is beginning to mold and sculpt, as it were, the highlights. You are creating forms while allowing those highlights to blend into the dark areas. From there go to the other corner of the same eye and scumble the highlight down in a fine long shape alongside the nose while allowing for a thin shadow between the highlight and the outline of the nose itself.

Step 5. After you have done this for the cheeks on both sides of the face, let both cheeks dry, and then do the nose, scumbling your way down from the bridge at the top of the nose to the bulb-shaped form at the bottom of the nose. Remember to do each nostril on either side of the tip. (See fig. 5.2.)

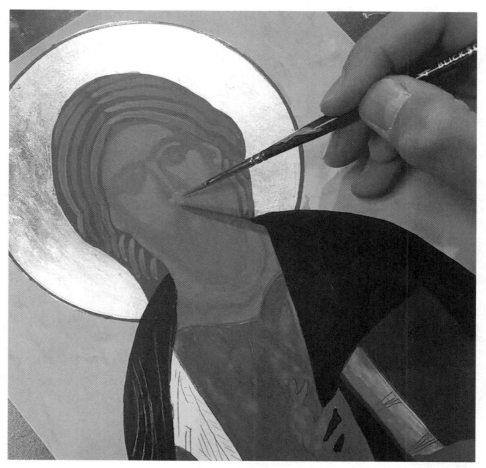

figure 5.2

Step 6. Now move on to the forehead. If you continue to think of the highlights as individual forms connected to a unified whole, you will be less daunted and more able to attend to them one at a time without being overwhelmed. For example, see the forehead as an inverted bowl with highlights on the dead center and fanning outward to disappear into the shadows on the edges. They are not separate forms pieced together as though they have been cut out of paper; they are forms that blend from light into darkness. Therefore, scumble the forehead by starting in the center and making even strokes moving outward.

Step 7. Let the forehead dry, clean your small brush thoroughly, and dry it. With the same brush and pigment, you will now paint, but not scumble, two neat and smooth highlights on the eyelids. Use as little pigment as possible, as the eyelids are small areas and you want just the lids to stand out of the shadows surrounding the eyes. In the same way, paint but do not scumble the visible parts of the left and right ears (use your color photograph to see what areas of the ear are visible), leaving a small shadow for the opening of the ear canal.

Step 8. From there, move on to the neck. Here we will return to the scumbling in order to achieve the gradual move from light to shadow. Note that there is a fine horizontal line in the neck, separating it in two parts in order to give the impression of a creased shadow. On the left side of the icon, the neck is visible all the way up to the ear. On the

right, the neck is obscured by the beard in order to give the impression that the head is slightly turned. Begin to form the beard by scumbling around the lower curve of it to make that area the brightest part and then scumbling down toward the crease. (See fig. 5.3.)

figure 5.3

Scumble the paint down the left side of the neck and then expand the scumbling into the wide area that forms the upper part of the neck. Leave a small line of separation to form the shadow between the two creases, and then do the same for the lower section, scumbling the paint from the brightest point in the center and out toward the edges.

Step 9. The last, and admittedly most challenging, part of the body to paint is the hands, but they are the most symbolically rich area. In our Judeo-Christian tradition, the hands play an integral part in the order of the spiritual realm. From the earliest books of scripture, we see hands being used to impart blessing, heal, and bring forth miracles—gestures and movements used especially and repeatedly by Jesus in his ministry. When we speak of creation, we say that it comes forth from the "hand of God."

Artistically, the hands have always proved problematic, and from medieval stained glass to Renaissance art and beyond, the hands were always reserved for the master artist to create. Such is the complex and daunting history of the hands. In fact, when I told a woman who had taken my workshop once that it would be nice for her to return for the following one, she said, "It depends . . . Are there any hands in this image?" However, don't let this frighten you away.

The symbolic richness of the hands in your icon is further enriched with the gesture Jesus makes with his right hand. As we said back on our first day, icons came to maturity during a time of the heresies, which questioned the divinity and humanity of Jesus. Icons are didactic, meaning they teach us, and this can be seen in some of their visual declarations of Christian truths. If you look at Jesus' hands, he holds two fingers up while joining the remaining three. The two upraised symbolize the two natures of his person, human and divine, while the three joined symbolize the Trinitarian nature of the Godhead. Even in the silent depths of the icon, Jesus himself declares: "I AM."

With this understanding and reverence for the hands and their gestures, take your clean small brush and the same lighter flesh pigment and begin to scumble the highlights on the right hand. First add the highlights on each finger, leaving a shadow line between the

figure 5.4

figure 5.5

figure 5.6

knuckles, fingertips, the palm, thumb area, and even the fingernails. Do the same for the left hand, which holds the book. It is not as complex as the blessing hand but still needs scumbling to bring the value up. (See fig. 5.4.)

Step 10. When you have finished all the flesh areas, let the pigment dry completely, and begin the process over again and repeat with scumbling at least three to four more times in order to lay down a solid foundation. (See fig. 5.5.) Let each coat dry before adding the next one. However, remember that you are not only building up the value of the color but also constantly molding and shaping the forms. As the drying time will decrease with each layer, and your rhythm will increase with your confidence, the succeeding layers will not take as long to apply as it did for me to describe them the first time. (See fig. 5.6.)

Step 11. Before closing our day with the garments and book, we want to take our thin fine liner brush (the smallest you have with the dagger point) and do the first linear work on the face and hair. With the steadiness and intentionality of purpose you have acquired with the tracing, incising, and now painting, you are ready for the precise poetry required for your facial lines. Keep your focus steady and your hesitation in check, and all will be well. Feel free to take a piece of scrap paper and practice the calligraphy of your lines; get a feeling for making a smooth, crisp line or undulating lines like water, going from thick to thin to thick again.

Step 12. In a clean palette cup, add a very small amount of Burnt Umber, no more than two to three drops, and with the tip of your liner brush add a very small dollop of Black, since it is a highly concentrated pigment and will dominate any color into which it is introduced. Add one to two drops of water (you don't want the paint too thin—again, the consistency of heavy cream is best). (See fig. 5.7.)

figure 5.7

Step 13. Get a fine sharp point on the tip of your brush with your fingers or, if the brush is clean, with your mouth as I do, and dip only the tip into the paint. With a smooth and steady hand, outline the eyeballs, but do not fill them in, and then the eyelashes, both top and bottom. Then put a very thin line defining the shadows under the eyes that separate them from the highlights on the cheeks. (See fig. 5.8.)

figure 5.8

Step 14. You want to next paint in the eyebrows, going from thin on the outside to slightly thicker on the inside; do this several times to get a nice and dark reading. Then do a complete outline of the nose, going down from the outside of the bridge on the top, all the way down and under the nostrils, tip, and then up again on the other side.

NOTE: These lines are meant to be ultrathin and very gentle, not thick globs of lines. Keep a light touch, and let your lines whisper rather than shout.

Step 15. Outline the ears and the folds around the ear canal. Then draw an extremely thin line to separate the lips as well as another very thin line under the bottom lip.

Step 16. For Jesus' beard we want the dark base coat to act as the foundation, but we will give a few linear strokes to convey the impression of hair. For the mustache, do not paint a single block of pigment, but paint four to five graceful and flowing lines on top of each other to create the two sides of the mustache. To create the beard itself, do not attempt to paint every strand, but begin with a thin outline of the sides of the beard, as seen in your color photograph, to define the shape, and move inward with thin, flowing, side-by-side lines to make it look like flowing hair. Make sure that these are not straight, but fluid, wavy organic lines. At this point, your lines should be fine because, unlike the highlights, we do not want to continually repeat the application but leave them as they are for now.

Step 17. We will close our day with the garments and the book. The red tunic will be first, since it is underneath everything else, and we want to create all the layers in an organic fashion. Into the red garment base that you already have in your palette, add three to four drops of Yellow Oxide and one drop of Titanium White. Yellow will predominate the highlights at this point, since we want the red to increase in luminosity, and simply adding white will only make it pink. Bear in mind that for the garments we will not be scumbling but doing more or less straight linear work to build up our highlights. Mix the pigment well, and add a few drops of water to achieve a heavy-cream consistency.

Step 18. Use your medium round painting brush, well cleaned and dry, for the first garment highlights. Before laying down any pigment, however, look carefully at your color photograph as well as the lines you have incised on your panel. See the configuration of the highlights in the garments, how the highlight lines begin on the side of the shadow as a slightly lighter color and then end with an almost pure white highlight on the top of that, each successive highlight getting smaller as it gets brighter. As with the face, the garments would resemble a pyramid if seen from the side or in 3-D.

Bring the first highlight down in a straight line along the dark shadow at the neck of the tunic, repeating the process down alongside the royal band over the shoulder, which we will attend to next. From there paint a highlight line along the folds of the tunic on the upper arm, and repeat on the sleeve of the blessing arm. (See fig. 5.9.) As the

figure 5.9

arm holding the book is covered with the outer cloak, you do not have to worry about red highlights there. Reinforce the first red highlights several times, getting thinner and smaller with the lines as you go.

Step 19. Without knowing it, you have incised the lines for the royal band over the shoulder, symbolizing authority and power. Look at your color guide photograph and see where the golden band is placed. In a clean palette cup, put three drops of Yellow Oxide and one drop of Burnt Umber, mix well with water if needed (to achieve heavy cream), and lay down several base coats of the yellowish-brownish mixture with your small round brush as the foundation for the band of royalty. (See fig. 5.10.) We will add the stripes later.

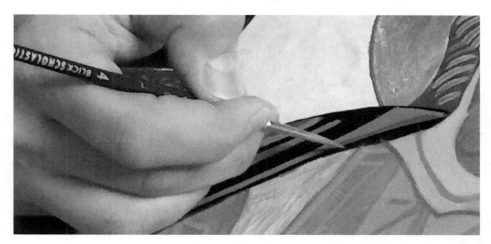

figure 5.10

Step 20. After you have reinforced the first red highlights several times, wash your medium brush, and turn your attention to the blue outer garment known in Greek as the *himation*. Into your blue foundation, saved from the previous day, add three drops of Titanium White, mix thoroughly, and add your water to achieve the heavy-cream consistency. Although the paint may initially appear to be too bright when you mix it thoroughly, remember that acrylic paints will dry darker than they appear when they are applied.

Step 21. If you look carefully at your photo, you will see that while on the himation the highlight principle is the same as it is on the red garment, there are a bit more rounded forms and organic movements as it drapes over the roundness of the shoulder. Short lines fan out from the inside of elliptical forms or connect between two parallel lines like ladders. It is a wild and almost surreal configuration of light and shadow that, more like sculpture than painting, is unlike any other rendering of fabric in art. Like the red highlights, make your first layer of blue highlights the widest, whether it is a straight line down the front

or an oval-shaped highlight on the shoulder. (See fig. 5.11.) The next will be thinner but brighter, and so on, as though you are laying down a wide lasagna noodle, followed by a medium-size fettucini noodle down the middle of the lasagna noodle, with a thin strand of spaghetti on top of them all. If that does not help clarify the point, it will at least make you hungry. We are nearly finished for the day, and the dinner bell will soon ring.

figure 5.11

Step 22. For the book, you will want to clean your medium-size brush well, dry it, and then take your Yellow Oxide and mix three drops into the brown you used for the book base color, saved from the previous day. Add water as need to achieve a heavy-cream consistency.

Since you used so little, the pigment from the previous day may have dried. In that case, simply add into a clean palette cup one-half Yellow Oxide and one-half Burnt Umber with a small dollop of Cadmium Red.

Step 23. With this pigment, paint three to four base coats on the book, paying attention to the sharp, crisp outlines. As you did before, use the incised lines of the outer edges as your irrigation ditches, pushing the paint directly to the outer incised lines and letting it neatly fall into the previously cut troughs.

Step 24. For the red pages of the book, mix three-fourths Cadmium Red with one-fourth Yellow Oxide into a clean palette cup, adding water as needed for the heavy-cream consistency.

Step 25. With a clean, dry medium brush, apply the paint three to four times over the pages, letting it dry between each application. Again, pay close attention to the crisp outside lines. (See fig. 5.12.)

Step 26. Clean your work station for the day. Add a few drops of water to each of the mixtures in your palette cups, and cover them well to ensure that they do not dry up. Wash your brushes thoroughly in soap and warm water.

• • •

Now, examine your icon. Look closely at what you have done, noting both what you have done well and what may need attention and more intentionality the next day. Most importantly, you can see how far you have come on your journey since first beginning as a novice iconographer. Look at everything you have made, and you will find it very good.

figure 5.12

And there was evening and there was morning, the fifth day.

Day 6

THE TRANSFIGURED ONE

So God created humankind in his image,
in the image of God he created them;
male and female he created them.

~Genesis 1:27

When I was a novice in the monastery (apparently the time and place for many a revelatory and transformative moment in my life), the senior monks took us juniors out to the Southwest in order to visit another monastery in New Mexico. Along the way we were also able to do some camping in the mountains and deserts of Colorado and Arizona, a pastime that had curiously eluded me in my decidedly urban and suburban upbringing.

One of the highlights was seeing the Grand Canyon, an experience that as both a newly minted novice and an inveterate urbanite, I never expected to have. We arrived at the South Rim of the Canyon just around sunset on a beautiful, clear, and excessively warm June evening. Twenty-some years of cowboy movies, textbook photos, and countless covers of *Arizona Highways* magazines had not prepared me for the breathtaking reality of what unfolded before me. The sun, just about to set over the horizon, was surrounded by a chromatic fantasy of reds, blues, pinks, purples, and every variation in between as though painted on the darkening sky.

Far below us, we could barely see the mighty Colorado River as it snaked its way nearly two miles down on the floor of the Canyon. The rocky walls, in fact, dropped so precipitously far below our feet that we actually looked down on pockets of thunderstorms, lightning flashing within the clouds like a flickering night light. As we reluctantly turned away from this cosmic kaleidoscope to return to our camper, we passed a woman standing there with tears in her eyes, gazing upon the same wondrous sight we had just left. "Who can ever say that there is no God," she said to her husband, unaware of our presence or the fact that we overheard her breathless remark.

Theological Reflection

Early in our journey we recalled the words of St. Paul when he said that Jesus is "the image [Greek: *eikon*] of the invisible God" (Col 1:15). We understood this to be a declaration, an affirmation of Jesus' perfect and sinless participation in the Father's substance and glory. Jesus is truly human, truly divine.

However, from that right and proper starting point, we have moved with John of the Cross into the Dark Night, obscuring what was previously clear and understandable, trusting in more than our fallible senses, and being led by faith alone. While mastering this technique is ongoing, we have hopefully begun to embrace the process of understanding light in a new way. The icon slowly reveals to us, like the process of creating one, the long and arduous process of transformation from exterior light to an interior one that shines forth when we follow Jesus and embrace the will of God. When our transformation, gifted by the Spirit, comes about, then we become like our first parents and are made new as images—icons—of the living God.

From the ascendancy of Byzantium to the present day, Eastern Christians have steadfastly held to icons as the purest theological manifestations of faith in a visual form. In the West, however, intellectual, religious, and socioeconomic changes brought about a divergence from the iconography, which from Constantinople in Asia Minor to Ravenna in Italy was pretty much the common language of Christian art until the thirteenth century. Beginning around the time of Cimabue, Giotto, and Duccio in the thirteenth century, sacred art took a monumental leap in a direction that reflected the recovery of classical humanism and laid the foundations for the coming Italian Renaissance. Realistic and proportional figures, driven by emotions and placed in naturalistic settings, began to slowly replace the static, flat, and ethereal language of the Eastern icon. Not only was the sacred divinity of Christ exalted and celebrated in art but—with no little influence from St. Francis with his stigmata, Stations of the Cross, and living Nativity scenes—Christ's sacred humanity was as well.

In one realm, however, the West continued in the iconographic theology of illumination from within as opposed to a light source from without. This was manifested in the glories of the magnificent stained-glass windows that soared in cathedrals, monasteries, and country churches from Florence to the Baltic regions.

Even today, walking into such medieval masterpieces as Notre Dame, Chartres, and Rheims, we are overawed by how stone and glass force us to reconfigure our concepts of space, time, and light. If they still have the power to awe and amaze us sophisticates of such a hypertechnologized age, imagine the effect on men and women eight hundred years ago who never saw any building larger than their neighbor's barn. Stained glass was intended to be more than a dazzling light show or a blazing chromatic tableaux intended to wow the unwashed masses. On the contrary, they were highly complex icons that employed glass, lead, and color to convey the same intrinsic truths about divinization and transformation as traditional icons. Images of the holy men and women in salvation history not only part the veil of time and reveal a glimpse of the coming glory of the kingdom of God, but they also show us the effects of sanctifying grace in our individual and communal lives.

Whether we follow the trail east toward Byzantine iconography or west toward cathedrals and stained glass, we arrive at the same scriptural event that becomes the converging point of both traditions. The Transfiguration—that moment on Mount Tabor when Jesus suddenly radiates a dazzling light before Peter, James, and John—ultimately becomes for us the meaning of what iconography is all about. Not only do we behold the glory of the Son, but also through our baptismal immersion into the life of Christ, we are transformed by the Spirit and like Christ become conduits of God's light.

For centuries, theologians have pondered the depths of the Transfiguration on Tabor, and one of the questions central to the whole inquiry is: What exactly did the disciples see when Jesus was transfigured? Any time Church dogma is debated in an open forum, it rarely brings about universal accord and oceans of bonhomie but, on the contrary, creates controversy and charges and countercharges of heresy.

Such was the case in the fourteenth century when the Eastern Orthodox cleric St. Gregory of Palamas spiritually linked the Transfiguration with the ancient form of prayer known as Hesychasm. Hesychasm, which is Greek for "silence" and "quietness," is a practice that goes back to the time of the Church Fathers and the first monks and nuns of the Syrian and Egyptian deserts of the third and fourth centuries. Hesychasm is not simply the absence of noise or abstaining from speech. It is a stilling, a quieting of the soul, a calming of the passions, disturbances, and disorders deep within us that drive us into sin, misery, and discontent and away from the will of God and the movement of the Spirit. It is also inextricably linked to the magnificent simplicity of the "Jesus Prayer" ("Lord Jesus Christ, have mercy on me, a sinner"), that early form of meditation in which one focuses on the name of Jesus as a mantra, which takes us deeper and deeper into union with the heart of the Lord.

St. Gregory believed, and defended the belief against his adversaries, that what the disciples saw on Mount Tabor was not simply a bright light radiating from Jesus that was blinding to behold. What they saw, Gregory said, was actually the energies (Greek: *dynameia*) of God: the power, majesty, glory, and beauty of God and a manifestation of the grace of the Spirit that dwells in our souls at Baptism. This energy made visible was, Gregory said, the closest mortals could come to see God while not seeing God's essence, which is impossible before the heavenly Beatific Vision.

Gregory also taught (and here is where the trouble began) that by virtue of our baptism in Christ, we share in his life and thus are capable of achieving the same sort of interior illumination—and one of the ways to do so is through Hesychastic prayer. When our passions and disordered desires that lead us away from original innocence are stilled when we obey God's will for us, we ourselves are filled with the ineffable light of grace. Through this life of silent prayer, charity, and outpouring of self for God and others, the void inside does not remain a void but is filled with God's light, which will shine out for all to see. This is what happened on Tabor to Jesus, this is what happened to the disciples, and, Gregory said, this is what can happen for us.

Unlike meditation, where enlightenment and peace is achieved through the focus of our will and the power of our concentration, the light of Hesychastic prayer is an unmerited gift of the Spirit that deepens our total union with God through Christ. While this light is not of our own doing or for our glory but God's alone, the fruits are tangible and sweet beyond all telling. Since we now live for God's will and commandments alone, a deep and unutterable peace descends upon and remains in our souls. No matter what trial or tribulations or calamities come our way, we are free from fear, anxiety, or passion, and we live entirely for and with our Beloved. As the song goes, this little light is going to shine.

● ○ ●

Painting the Icon

Materials for Day 6

- Painting brushes:
  - #4 medium round brush
  - #10 small round brush
  - Fine dagger-point liner brush
- Liquid acrylic paints (1 ounce each):
  - Yellow Oxide
  - Raw Umber
  - Titanium White
  - Cadmium Red
  - Burnt Umber
  - Black
  - Prussian Blue
  - Yellow Ochre
- Plastic palette with at least 6 to 8 "wells"
- Squirt bottle filled with water
- Clean rags
- Plastic wrap

Steps for Day 6

To apply the final layers of pigment to our icon, we are going to simply repeat the steps of the last day's highlighting. However, we will go several values higher in smaller concentrated areas of light. The intensity of these brighter and smaller applications will not only continue to round off and give more form to the face and garments, but it will also take us further down the road to our goal of interior illumination.

Step 1. Begin with the face, and remember that the flesh (face, neck, and hands) and beard are the only portions of the icon on which we will use the scumbling technique. Uncover your pigments from the previous day, and add two drops of Titanium White to your palette cup with the leftover flesh pigment. With the tip of your small round painting brush, pick up a smidgen of Cadmium Red, and mix it into your paint to warm up the tone a bit. Make sure there is enough water left, or add some, to get the consistency of milk (instead of heavy cream). With the same brush, mix the paint thoroughly and get all the excess paint off the lip of the cup.

Step 2. With the same brush, with just a small amount of paint so that the brush is almost dry, begin your scumble at the brightest point of the left cheek bone directly under the bottom of the eye shadow. Begin your scumbling, and work your way down but not as far as your last highlight, letting the pigment run out toward the bottom but concentrated on top. Since there is more water than before, the paint will take a bit longer to dry, so let it be, and move on to the highlight on the other side of the eye next to the nose, using the same technique of stumbling your highlight down in the same way. Then go up to the forehead and work your way with your semidry brush from the center and out to all the edges near the hair, allowing the highlight to disappear into the shadows. Do several highlights above the eyes, leaving a small shadow of separation between them and the forehead. Do the same on the other cheeks and then the nose, scumbling from the brightest part on the bridge and letting the paint run out toward the bulblike tip of the nose. Then, give a real jolt to the nose by painting a large dollop of highlight on the tip. Do the same on the ear lobes, and then scumble with your nearly dry brush a highlight from the lightest points on the neck down to the crease in the middle; then start again with a scumbled highlight down to the collar of the garment. (See fig. 6.1.)

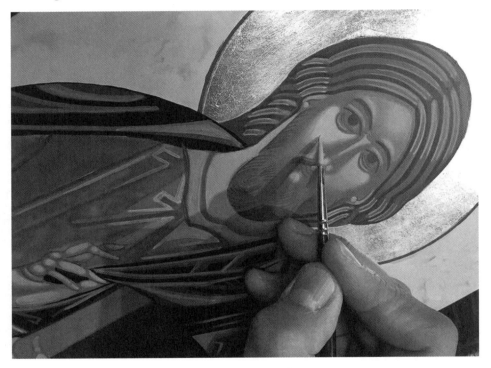

figure 6.1

Step 3. When you have finished the facial area, move down to the hands, and with your fine liner brush and the same new lighter flesh pigment, do the last scumbled highlights. Remember that the high-lights on the hand, like the face, will emerge more clearly when you see them as individual parts of a whole, separated by shadows that radiate their own light. Gently scumble a highlight on each section of each finger, allowing a shadow in between them. Scumble the middle of the palm, and move outward. Remember to get the wrist as well. Move to the other hand, and pay particular attention to the knuckles and the individual fingers as they disappear around the book they hold. (See fig. 6.2.)

Step 4. Before moving on to the garments, we want to reinforce the highlights on the hair, subtly, so we don't make them too bright or over-powering. Take your leftover dark brown base that you used for the hair's foundation, and add three to four drops of Yellow Ochre and a few drops of water, to achieve the consistency of heavy cream, and stir well. With your clean and dry medium brush, and bearing in mind our concept for the hair of imagining spaghetti on top of fettucini on top of lasagna noodles, paint your final and thinner highlights down the center of the last ones. Allow each line to dry before applying the next one on top of it. Keep this process particularly organic, and let your brush gently follow the fluid lines of the hair, allowing

figure 6.2

the line to flow down the side of Jesus' head, around the ears, and then over the tight curls that flow behind his shoulder.

Step 5. On the red tunic, look and see how your first highlights separated the light from the shadow and created your forms. Like you did on the facial highlights, so you will also do for the garments, only you will be painting instead of scumbling. This time, add two to three small drops of Titanium White to your leftover red pigment mixture and two to three drops of water, for heavy-cream consistency, and mix well.

Step 6. Find the light edge of the former highlight as your starting point. Dip the tip of the small round painting brush, clean and semidry, and add a thinner line on the outside of your last highlight (your color photograph proves invaluable at this time). For example, where there is a highlight line on the front of the tunic, paint a thinner and brighter line; where there is a triangular fold such as there is at the top near the neck, paint a smaller and brighter triangle within; and where you did a large square U around the folds on the forearm, do another but smaller. (See fig. 6.3.)

figure 6.3

Step 7. Now we will do the same with the blue himation. Again, add two to three small drops of Titanium White to your leftover blue pigment mixture and two to three drops of water, for heavy-cream consistency, and mix well.

Step 8. Take your small brush, clean and semidry, and apply the blue paint mixture. Following the color photograph, add thinner highlight lines outside the previous ones.

Step 9. On the golden band over Jesus' shoulder, symbolizing his kingship, you have already laid down a neutral base with your mixture of one drop Burnt Umber and three drops of Yellow Oxide. If you look at the color photograph, you will see that there is one layer of highlight, and that consists of a series of gold striation marks of varying length, width, and direction to give the effect of gold radiating outward. The original icon would undoubtedly have had actual gold on the band, but for our intents and purposes we will use a similar combination of what we used for our background in order to achieve a faux-gold effect. If you do not have any of the paint remaining from when you did the background, mix a small amount of Yellow Oxide (about one-half of the palette cup) with Titanium White (about one-half of the palette cup), with a dollop of the greenish Raw Umber. Stir well, and add water as needed to achieve a heavy-cream consistency.

Step 10. With your fine liner brush, paint the zigging and zagging striation lines, following your color guide photograph. Do so several times to increase their intensity, allowing each layer to dry before applying the next lines on top.

Step 11. Remembering that iconography is a series of expansions and contractions, we go once again from large color fields (expansion) to fine line work to tighten things up and bring them together (contraction). Using your fine liner brush, add Burnt Umber (brown) to fill up a clean palette cup halfway, and add a tiny dollop of Black, and mix well, adding water until it looks like heavy cream.

Step 12. With a very fine and steady hand, reinforce and redefine the eyebrows, eye lashes, the thin line separating the hair from the flesh, the lines outside the head, and a very, very fine series of scumbled thin lines suggesting wisps of hair in the mustache and beard.

Step 13. When you have finished the linear reinforcements, take a small bit of the same brown mixture that you just used, and lighten it with just a touch Yellow Oxide.

Step 14. Carefully color each eye brown, as seen in the color photograph, since Jesus' Middle Eastern blood would definitely have given him brown eyes instead of the blue eyes depicted by Hollywood and in holy cards. A small black dot in the center of the brown will suffice for work on the eyes.

figure 6.4

Step 15. For the final highlights on the flesh, take your fine liner brush and with Titanium White put three thin, sharp slashes on the left top of the left cheek on the brightest part of the highlight, and then do the same under the eye on the same side next to the nose. (See fig. 6.4 .) Do the same on the right cheek and under the right eye, and then put three more on the forehead, two above each eyebrow, one on the tip of the nose, a dot on the ears, three lines on the center of the neck below the beard and two under the shadow, and then a few on the palms, knuckles, and fingers of each hand. See the color photograph for guidance. Even with such small, nearly imperceptible white highlights on the flesh, you will be surprised how the intensity of the face and hands will treble.

Step 16. The last thing we want to do on the face before our final day is to create the lips. You want the lips to be red in order to warm the face up a bit, but not to the extent where they overpower and distract. We want warmth but not ruby red. To achieve this, mix three-fourths Cadmium Red with one-fourth Burnt Umber brown. Stir well, and add a drop of water to achieve the consistency of heavy cream.

Step 17. With your fine liner brush, gently paint in the top lip and then paint in the bottom lip. Two to three coats should suffice (allowing each to dry before applying the next one) in order to get the depth and richness desired. When all the coats are dried, add a small dollop of Titanium White to your lip mixture, and paint the bottom lip several times with this brighter value in order to give a sense of separation and variation to the mouth.

Step 18. Clean your work station for the day. Add a few drops of water to each of the mixtures in your palette cups, and cover them well to ensure that they do not dry up. Wash your brushes thoroughly in soap and warm water.

● ● ●

We have now nearly completed our image, and our exertions are beginning to shine forth as clearly as the light from the panel itself. Night draws near, and the day of rest approaches. Look at your panel, especially in light of how far you have come in so short a time. See how good it is.

And there was evening and there was morning, the sixth day.

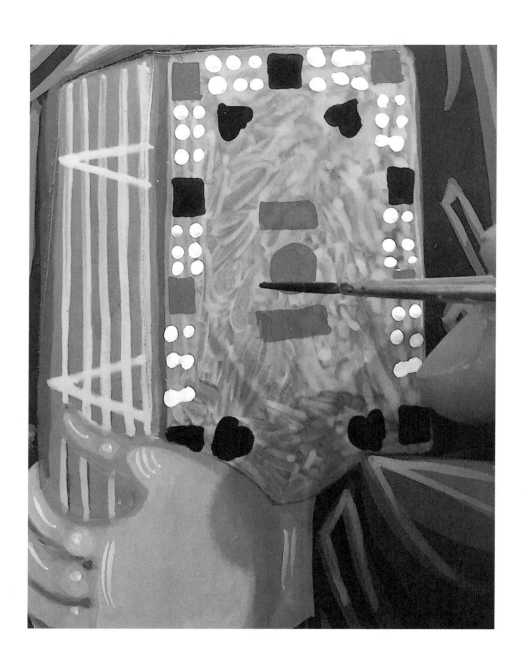

Day 7

UNITY IN COMMUNITY

*So God blessed the seventh day
and hallowed it, because on it God rested
from all the work he had done in creation.*

~Genesis 2:3

When I was first invited to be the artist in residence at St. Gregory the Great Parish by the former pastor, Fr. Bart, I gratefully and excitedly accepted. A moment later, however, I paused and with a furrowed brow asked, "What does that mean?" Fr. Bart shot back, "I don't know, but let's figure it out." Despite my enthusiasm, I was, to be frank, out to sea, or wandering in a dark wood. Choose whatever metaphor you like, I was lost.

Happily, I can say that fifteen years and hundreds of icons later, I am still adrift and lost in a dark wood—as I am about most of what unfolds in my life—but at least I have a somewhat better sense of purpose and direction. Most importantly, at St. Gregory I have been given the greatest gift of my vocation: a community. The community, led first by Fr. Bart and now by Fr. Paul and our associate Fr. Brian, has not simply given me a place to hang my apron and do my work on a daily basis. Even though I am immensely and eternally grateful for the studio space and the silence and solitude it gives me to create my work, the community has also given me love and support and encouragement. The community represents the people I serve and offers me the joy of being answerable and responsible to others, all the while being challenged to change and better, not only my work, but my life of prayer as well. What the community offers me is relationship, which—with all its joys and frustrations, agonies and ecstasies, wounds and healings—is like water in the desert.

The most difficult lesson that I had to learn (and one I continue to learn) was how to cease thinking and acting in one way and begin thinking and acting in another. What Fr. Bart and then Fr. Paul and Fr. Brian all taught me by their examples as priests-as-servants in the community was that I could not shoehorn iconography into my life simply as an adjunct or, worse, a career. What they taught me was that iconography, especially as I came to dwell in the St. Gregory community, was not a job but something God had called me to do, not so much with my life, but as my life. This gift was a calling meant not to serve my own artistic fulfillment but to deepen my relationship with God and to serve the Church, by which is not meant stone and mortar but flesh-and-blood people. What they were teaching me, first by the example of their own lives, was the difference between a career and a vocation. A career we choose for whatever amount of time we like. A vocation chooses us for a substantially longer period of time—in fact, our whole life.

Theological Reflection

Embracing the vocation of iconography by working within and for the Church entailed unlearning—as I said earlier—previously held ideas and misconceptions, and entering by faith alone into new ones. I had to give up the good old Yankee American idea of hard work as five days of performing and producing. A nine-to-five routine of getting my legs under my desk and producing simply to earn a paycheck was done—over and out. My vocation had to have a holistic reality, and it had to fill every nook and cranny of my being like air.

Aside from my actual icon painting, book writing, restoration, and preparing for lectures, workshops, and retreats—perusing through books and sketching became my work. Pausing for an hour and walking to the beach in the summer, or strolling through the tree-lined neighborhood in fall, or staring silently at the rooftops of Andersonville from the window of my third-floor studio all became work. Silent and solitary visits to churches, museums, and art exhibits or moments of prayer or reading in front of an icon for a half hour all became part of my work as well. As long as it is an action that feeds my creativity and opens my heart to the movements of the Spirit, it is all part of my vocation. However, if I sit on the couch with potato chips and the remote, doing nothing, then I am nothing but a bum, wasting my time and God's.

I do not want to sound as though I am trumpeting my particular vocation, as though I have been called to some lofty ecclesiastical Mount Olympus. I have not. We are all called by God to a vocation in this life, which means an awareness of our *be*-ing with God and for others and not simply a mindless *do*-ing for ourselves. When I have given workshops, lectures, and church tours over the years, I speak about how we think and act when encountering sacred space and images. People immediately think they need to learn how to process the meaning of this encounter in order to understand it. I say that they are half right because in order to understand the encounter they need to recover the understanding of this language, this thinking and acting in the presence of the sacred, which is already embedded in their spiritual DNA.

Even though the working class has borne the heaviest burden since the building of the pyramids, it was only after the Industrial Revolution, a mere 175 years ago, that we lost a truly supernatural component of our existence. Even though there are no sweeping historical absolutes because history is extraordinarily layered and textured, it can be said that the Industrial Revolution was the spiritual game changer that separated us from what and who were meant to be. Before tens of thousands of men and women were concentrated in urban tenements to fuel the interminable output of the industrial beast, they lived a fairly agrarian or simple urban existence centered on their family and their community. They were tied to the land, to the fields, to the forests, to the lakes and rivers. They were tied to their church and to each other. They were not called to work or told the time of day or year by a steam whistle or clock; they looked at the sun, the moon, and the stars. They felt the wind, smelled the air, watched the tide, and listened to the parish church bells. They did not work twelve- and fourteen-hour days in factories or vast warehouses to supply the needs of a world market, but reaped enough harvest, dressed enough venison, and made enough silver goods to feed their families and their community.

When they walked into the great cathedrals of Chartres, Notre Dame, Rheims, and Lincoln, they did not need docents and guide books to explain the magnificence and splendor of the space. Their organic connectedness to the earth and the architecture of nature allowed them to read and understand the portals, the font, the long nave, and the rose window. They could look up into the vaults at the massive image of the Virgin and Child and understand the Misericordia (Heart of Mercy) and the crucified Christ and enter into the heart of suffering—the heart of the One who united himself with our feeble humanity. It was intuition seamlessly melded into everyday life experience.

My intention here is not to romanticize and gild what was obviously a time of great poverty, widespread disease, and injustice. Our forebears were not divinized gnostics who had singlehandedly unlocked the secrets of the universe. On the contrary, they were simply people like us who nevertheless had a heightened awareness of the world around them and understood their place in that world. This is not New Age folderol or mystical mumbo jumbo but our natural condition, our natural relationship with God and that which lies buried in the compost of our frantic, fragmented, and technologized lives. It is this connectedness to ourselves, others, and the world around us that we need to recover. That is how we remain at rest, which is another name for peace, even in the midst of our day-to-day lives.

This is what I imagine that God did when he rested on the seventh day after all the exertions of creation. He did not crawl into a celestial hammock or curl up in the shade of a cosmic oak tree, but simply gloried in the pure act of being. Similarly, when we recover our sense of vocation, our sense of what God wants us to not so much do but be, the transformation will begin. We will rest in our *be*-ing, and John of the Cross's "Ray of Darkness" will shine in our hearts like the light of Tabor. On fire with that light, we will come to know that we live our lives in God, in unity with Jesus and in community with others.

● ● ●

Painting the Icon

Materials for Day 7

- Painting brushes:
  - #4 medium round brush
  - #10 small round brush
  - Fine dagger-point liner brush
- Liquid acrylic paints (1 ounce each):
  - Yellow Oxide
  - Raw Umber
  - Titanium White
  - Venetian Red
  - Cadmium Red
  - Burnt Umber
  - Black
  - Prussian Blue
  - Yellow Ochre
- Plastic palette with at least 6 to 8 "wells"
- Plastic or paper utility cups (about 3 ounces)
- Squirt bottle filled with water
- Clean rags
- Needle-pointed stylus or fine-tip incising tool
- Compass with painting nib
- Ruler
- Pencil
- Professional high-gloss artist's varnish

Steps for Day 7

Even though it is the day of rest, we will put the finishing touches on the icon, but they will be enjoyable and even fun and not too labor-intensive. As one of my many and legendary maxims go, the last 10 percent of work on the icon will punch it up 75 percent.

Step 1. The first of the last things to do is to use your saved mixture of Burnt Umber with a touch of Black, and with your thin liner brush, gently reinforce the linear elements: the eyes, eyebrows, hair lines, mustache, and beard, and then the outline of the blue himation and the book. On the red tunic you do not want to have a heavy and dark hand with the lines, but do put down a very thin line on the top of the tunic at the neck, lines on either side of the golden royal band, and then a line on the horizontal top of the forearm of the blessing hand as well as one on the sleeve at the wrist.

Step 2. For the highlights on the book pages, add Yellow Oxide to fill a clean pallet cup halfway, plus a small touch of Cadmium Red. Add water as needed to achieve a consistency of heavy cream. With a ruler and the painting nib of the compass used for the halo, carefully draw straight highlights down the side of the book, to look like pages.

Step 3. Then in the same way paint the triangular book clasps, using a mixture of pure Yellow Oxide (filling a clean pallet cup halfway, and adding water as needed to achieve the heavy-cream consistency) with a few dots of pure white to give the impression of metal. (See fig. 7.1.)

figure 7.1

figure 7.2

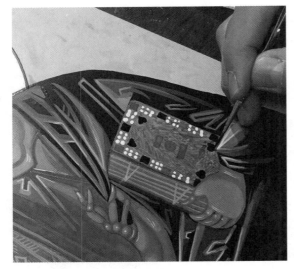

figure 7.3

figure 7.4

Step 4. The jewels on the book should be painted with the fine liner brush in a relatively straightforward manner so as not to be confused by their placement and execution. (See fig. 7.2.) Basically, each stone is a solid monochromatic image: use White for the pearls and vary between Cadmium Red and Prussian Blue for the round and rectangular jewels. Keep them geometrically placed, but don't try to measure each one in a perfectly precise manner. Keep them organic. (See fig. 7.3.)

Step 5. With your ruler and a pencil, measure and lightly draw in the cross inside Jesus' halo, with the lines fanning out at a short forty-five-degree angle where the cross lines meet the halo. See the color photograph for guidance. (See fig. 7.4.)

If you look closely, you will see that there are six single lines that form the cross, but there are three more, one to the right of the center vertical line, and another under the left and right horizontal lines. Be sure to add these as well.

There are only three arms of the cross visible, which again honors the Trinitarian nature of the Christian faith. (See fig. 7.5.)

Step 6. When the penciled lines are complete, do a mixture of Cadmium Red (filling a clean pallet cup halfway, and adding water as needed to achieve the heavy-cream consistency) with a dollop of Burnt Umber. Apply the mixture to the painting nib of your compass, and use the ruler to paint the nine lines of the cross. (See fig. 7.6.)

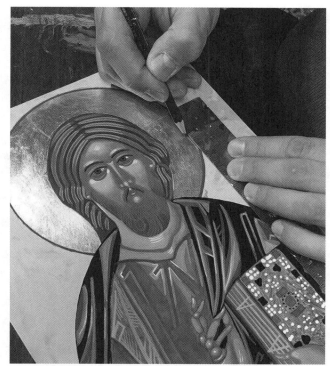

figure 7.5

figure 7.6

Step 7. With the same color and painting nib of your compass, inside Jesus' halo, you want to inscribe three Greek letters: *omega*, *omicron*, and *nu*, which will look like the letters O, W, N. (See figs. 7.7, 7.8, and 7.9.) In Greek, this translates into "The Being One" or "He Who Is"—the name that God revealed to Moses from the burning bush and that Jesus used in reference to himself ("I AM").

figure 7.7

figure 7.8

figure 7.9

Step 8. The last lettering you need to do is the initials of Jesus Christ that look like *IC XC* on either side of the halo. This is an abbreviation of the Greek name for Jesus, IHCOYC, and Christ, XPICTOC. Given the size of our panel, no more than an inch tall for each letter will suffice and read fine. Your color for the lettering will be the same red and brown you used for the halo, cross, and inner letters. Continue to use the painting nib of your compass. You will want to use your ruler to measure not only the height but also the spacing of the letters, which should be equidistant from the halo but allow at least a one-half inch from either side for the border. In order to see where your letters will be, put a light pencil line down, as it can be erased after the paint dries. (See fig 7.10.)

figure 7.10

Step 9. Our very last act of painting is to put the border around the icon. As with everything else we have done with our image, there is a deeper meaning beyond the surface reality. The border does not act as an aesthetic complement to the work, substituting for a frame to hold it together and make it visually pleasing. On the contrary, our border represents an aperture, a sacred doorway and window into the eternal realm through which we gaze. To create this border, take your Venetian Red and squeeze some into a clean utility cup, filling it up halfway, and adding water as needed to achieve a heavy-cream consistency.

Step 10. With your ruler and incising tool, measure and incise a one-fourth-inch border line on all four sides, going over the bottom part of the robe and up to the halo. This will allow Jesus to come forward through the icon and into our reality. Paint in the border with the Venetian Red using the small round painting brush; several layers should suffice, allowing each to dry between applications. When you have the border completed, turn the panel and paint all four edges of the panel in the same color, using a medium-size brush.

Step 11. After everything is dry, be sure to erase any remaining pencil markings.

Step 12. Clean your work station and wash your brushes thoroughly in soap and warm water. You can discard the leftover paints in the palette and wash it out.

Step 13. Jumping slightly ahead, please give your icon several days to dry, or "cure," and after that time you will be ready to varnish it. This is a process by which not only is the image sealed and protected from the damaging effects of dust, dirt, harmful light, and just plain and simple time, but also the luminosity of the colors will be punched up considerably. You want to use a professional artist's varnish, which can be purchased from any art store, and not an industrial polyurethane, which is much too strong and unsuitable for a piece of art. Remember to pick any paintbrush hairs out of the varnish as you paint it onto the icon, and apply it in a well-ventilated area and let it dry in the same.

• • •

It is appropriate that we have closed our journey with the painting of the doorway. It is a spiritually rich and full image of what we have attempted, and succeeded, to do over these past seven days. For six days, we have worked, prayed, thought, hesitated, moved forward, fallen back, and now have arrived at our destination. But that is only the beginning of the journey. It is now the seventh day; we are at rest and have opened the door to the Lord. Like the loving and compassionate father of the prodigal son, he will now come to meet us. Honor yourself.

And there was evening and there was morning, the seventh day.

Day 8

```
CONCLUSION

An end and a beginning.
```

One of the most important gifts we can develop in our spiritual life is the gift not only of listening but also of seeing. In our journey with the icon for the past seven days, we have learned that when both are combined—the active listening in our prayer and the active seeing in our work—what slowly emerges is what Flannery O'Connor called the "Habit of Being."

I hope you have taken away from this journey something more than how to apply gold leaf, mix and scumble paint, and clean your brushes. The process of painting an icon, like an icon itself, is merely a surface reality that leads you through a sacred doorway into deeper truths within that are waiting to be revealed. The process of painting ends at some point, but we continue to learn that both hearing and seeing have a deeper and more mystical reality beyond what we are taught about them by the world and our own senses.

Hearing does not simply mean listening for the ring of our cell phone, the ping of the incoming text, or the opening notes of our favorite songs queued up in our laptop. In the same way, seeing does not simply mean the reality we perceive through the screen of our computer, watching our favorite show, reading the current best seller, or beholding the gloominess or magnificence of a dark and rainy or warm and sunny morning. Hearing and seeing are—as we have explored through our journey with the great saints, poets, philosophers, and artists—more about the art of making your heart and your ears open to the presence of God in the everyday, ordinary ebb and flow of life.

Blind Homer saw deeper into the human experience than any other bard of the classical world. Helen Keller, denied the gifts of not only sight but also hearing and speech, went on to become one of the most respected, articulate, and influential women of the twentieth century. We would like to think this "inner sight" and "silent hearing" is something mystical and mysterious that we have to be initiated into like a secret society with a secret handshake and password. Like the search for God, we want to see earthquakes and lightning and hear heavenly choirs even though God is invariably a drifting cloud on the horizon and a whisper in the wind.

It is in the magnificence of the mundane where we find the most profound revelation of the sacred. If we have taken anything away from our pilgrimage, it is how to read an extraordinary sacred language in the most ordinary of guises. Like the peasant reading the cathedral, like the farmer listening to the breeze, or like us as we move beyond the doorway of the icon into a place deeper within where relationship begins, it is all simply seeing and listening with our hearts.

To illustrate this point and bring us to the last and most important step in our journey, I use the example of, of all things, a baptismal font or even a baptistery. As adults, chances are we have been to dozens of baptisms of children of family and friends. If we have been to Europe, we have visited the baptisteries of the great churches and cathedrals, such as Giotto's masterpiece across from the Duomo in Florence. However, have we taken note that the shape of the font or even the space itself is in the form of an octagon?

We have seen in the course of the past seven days that salvation history has revealed to us a sacred geometry, a numerology of faith in which numbers themselves become icons that manifest truth. The numbers three, seven, twelve, forty, and so forth all have a resonance that ring with deeper meaning, from the days of creation to our present time. The number eight symbolizes the day after creation and represents a new day, a rebirth, a new life. After our birth, even in our innocence as babies, we still carry the stain of original sin, that mark of death, bequeathed to us by our first parents. It is in the waters of Baptism, when we are immersed into the death and resurrection of Jesus, the New Adam, that the powers of sin and death are broken and we are reborn and made new. Therefore, it's appropriate that the baptismal font has eight sides to reflect this reality of newness and rebirth.

Obviously, the thought of treating the icon like a baby and plunging it into the depths of a baptismal font is neither practical nor even rational. However, we do want to invoke the blessings of the Spirit on the icon because it has now become a sacred image fostering prayer and is worthy of veneration. Remember: it is for veneration, not worship. This new life is imparted upon the icon in the form of a blessing, optimally within the context of the liturgy. The Eastern Orthodox form of blessing is to place the icon in the tabernacle for the forty days of Lent and have it emerge with the glory of the risen Christ on Easter morning. It is also possible to ask your priest to place the icon on the altar during Mass. This offers the additional blessing of having the rite of blessing of the icon performed during the liturgy in the presence of the assembly. However, practically speaking, every parish possesses the Book of Blessing, which contains the rites for all forms and manners of benedictions, ranging from blessing the sick to blessing new houses. You may ask your priest to perform the blessing of sacred images, which the book contains. The important thing, however, is the ritual itself more than its context, or where and when it's done.

● ● ●

We have now completed the journey. The icon has been blessed and imbued with the Spirit. Therefore, it is time to let it go since, in a manner of speaking, it is no longer yours—not in terms of actual possession, but in regard to why you created it in the first place. Like a child, created, nurtured, and raised, the icon must now be let go so that others can benefit from the light you worked so hard and diligently to let radiate from within. As my mother would say about her children: "First you give them roots, and then you give them wings." Like our faith, our icon was not meant to be clung to as our own personal property under our own little bushel. It must now be raised up as a light shining out for all to see.

And there was evening and there was morning, the eighth day.

Acknowledgments

A debt of gratitude is owed to so many people since this book has not materialized merely over the course of a year or two but is instead the fruit of nearly two decades of my vocation as an iconographer and artist-in-residence at St. Gregory the Great Church in Chicago. I would like to thank the pastor, Fr. Paul Wachdorf, the associate pastor, Fr. Brian Fischer, and all the staff and parishioners who have given me a home for my vocation as well as the support and encouragement needed for me to live that calling. Anna Marie Crovetti, my dear friend of a quarter of a century and fellow artist, not only shot the beautiful and evocative photographs for this book but also, with her professionalism and gentle guidance, pushed me forward and kept the process on track when I was ready to derail.

To Jonathan Weyer, my editor at Ave Maria Press, a special thanks is owed. Jonathan both provided the vision and inspiration for this book and also helped bring the dream to fruition with his wisdom, insight, and editorial acumen par excellence. I would also like to thank Tom Grady and the entire staff at Ave Maria Press for their belief in my work and invaluable assistance in putting it together in the book you now read.

Patrick Lyne, my friend and assistant at the Trinity Icons studio, helped me immensely with artistic, photographic, and graphic skills that are far beyond my ken. Not only did he assist me in managing and editing the text and photographs but he also kept the studio running smoothly so I could focus my time and attention on this project. Fr. Sergio Rivas of the Archdiocese of Chicago was kind enough to advise me on certain points of theology, especially in the realm of patristics and mystical theology.

Lastly, I would like to thank Bishop Robert Barron of Los Angeles. He has been a good friend and supporter of my work over many years, and his powerful and moving foreword went beyond the bounds of a mere introduction and stands as a Magnificat for all artists of faith.

Appendix

Materials Needed

Panel Preparation Utensils and Tools

- ❑ 8" x 10" white gessoed panel
- ❑ An 8"x 10" color copy and black-and-white copy of the Christ Pantocrator icon. You can obtain these images in two ways: (1) download and print both copies from the Ave Maria Press website at www.avemariapress.com/product/1-59471-757-5/Drawing-Closer-to-Christ/#more_tab, or (2) photocopy Plate V of the color insert of this book in color and in black and white at 150 percent of the original. You will not trace the border so be sure to trim it from your black-and-white image.
- ❑ Carbon paper
- ❑ Adhesive tape
- ❑ Steel wool
- ❑ Ballpoint pen with fine point or fine-tip drafting pencil
- ❑ Compass with interchangeable pencil and painting nib (available at an art supply store)
- ❑ Needle-pointed stylus or fine-tip incising tool
- ❑ Ruler

Gilding Materials and Utensils

- ❑ 4 or 5 sheets of gold leaf (real is best, but imitation will suffice)
- ❑ Gold size (gold-leaf glue)

Painting Materials and Utensils

- ❑ Extremely soft, imitation sable brush (for brushing, not painting)
- ❑ Utility brushes:

- ○ Medium round brush
- ○ Small flat utility brush
- ❑ Painting brushes:
  - ○ #8 large round brush
  - ○ #4 medium round brush
  - ○ #10 small round brush
  - ○ Fine dagger-point liner brush
- ❑ Liquid acrylic paints (1 ounce each):
  - ○ Venetian Red
  - ○ Cadmium Red
  - ○ Burnt Umber
  - ○ Yellow Oxide
  - ○ Raw Umber
  - ○ Titanium White
  - ○ Black
  - ○ Prussian Blue
  - ○ Yellow Ochre
- ❑ Plastic or paper utility cups (about 3 ounces)
- ❑ Squirt bottle filled with water
- ❑ Fine-grit sandpaper
- ❑ Plastic palette with at least 6 to 8 "wells"
- ❑ Clean rags
- ❑ Plastic wrap
- ❑ Scrap paper
- ❑ Pencil
- ❑ Professional high-gloss artist's varnish

These materials may be purchased at craft and art supply stores or online at these sites:
Blick Art Supplies (www.dickblick.com)
Michaels (www.michaels.com)
Pandora Iconographer's Supplies (www.iconboards.com)

Joseph Malham is an iconographer and artist-in-residence at St. Gregory the Great Catholic Church in Chicago, Illinois. He is the author of two books, including the award-winning *John Ford: Poet in the Desert*, and was the subject of an Emmy-winning religious interest story by WGN in Chicago in 2014. In 2015, Malham also was given the Archdiocese of Chicago Bishop Quarter Award, which honors lay Catholics for their service to the Archdiocese.

Malham attended St. Meinrad Seminary and Loyola University Chicago. He has contributed to *Liguorian, Faith & Form: An Interfaith Journal on Art & Architecture*, and the *Chicago Tribune*.

He may be reached at joe@trinityicons.com.